A LITTLE BOOK FOR

NEW PREACHERS

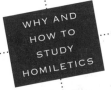

WHY AND
HOW TO
STUDY
HOMILETICS

MATTHEW D. KIM

ivp
Academic

An imprint of InterVarsity Press
Downers Grove, Illinois

InterVarsity Press
P.O. Box 1400, Downers Grove, IL 60515-1426
ivpress.com
email@ivpress.com

InterVarsity Press® is the book-publishing division of InterVarsity Christian Fellowship/
USA®, a movement of students and faculty active on campus at hundreds of universities,
colleges, and schools of nursing in the United States of America, and a member
movement of the International Fellowship of Evangelical Students. For information about
local and regional activities, visit intervarsity.org.

All Scripture quotations, unless otherwise indicated, are taken from The Holy Bible, New
International Version®, NIV®. Copyright © 1973, 1978, 1984, 2011 by Biblica, Inc.™ Used
by permission of Zondervan. All rights reserved worldwide. www.zondervan.com. The
"NIV" and "New International Version" are trademarks registered in the United States
Patent and Trademark Office by Biblica, Inc.™

Chapter 9, "Being Prayerful and Spirit-Led," has been adapted and expanded from an
article published as "The Preacher's Forgotten 'God': 3 Ways to Incorporate the Holy
Spirit in Our Preaching," Preaching Today, http://www.preachingtoday.com/skills/2017
/august/preachers-forgotten-god.html. Used by permission.

Cover design: Cindy Kiple
Interior design: Beth McGill

ISBN 978-0-8308-5347-2 (print)
ISBN 978-0-8308-7021-9 (digital)

Printed in the United States of America ∞

InterVarsity Press is committed to ecological stewardship and to the conservation of natural
resources in all our operations. This book was printed using sustainably sourced paper.

Library of Congress Cataloging-in-Publication Data
Names: Kim, Matthew D., 1977- author.
Title: A little book for new preachers : why and how to study homiletics / Matthew D. Kim.
Description: Downers Grove, IL : InterVarsity Press, 2020. | Series: Little books series |
    Includes bibliographical references and index.
Identifiers: LCCN 2019041596 (print) | LCCN 2019041597 (ebook) | ISBN 9780830853472
    (print) | ISBN 9780830870219 (digital)
Subjects: LCSH: Preaching.
Classification: LCC BV4211.3 .K5529 2020 (print) | LCC BV4211.3 (ebook) | DDC 251—dc23
LC record available at https://lccn.loc.gov/2019041596
LC ebook record available at https://lccn.loc.gov/2019041597

| P | 21 | 20 | 19 | 18 | 17 | 16 | 15 | 14 | 13 | 12 | 11 | 10 | 9 | 8 | 7 | 6 | 5 | 4 | 3 | 2 |
| Y | 37 | 36 | 35 | 34 | 33 | 32 | 31 | 30 | 29 | 28 | 27 | 26 | 25 | 24 | 23 | 22 | 21 |

TO SCOTT M. GIBSON

My mentor, friend, and colleague
who encouraged me to preach
and to study homiletics

■ ■ ■

CONTENTS

ACKNOWLEDGMENTS

■ ■ ■

MANY PEOPLE ARE DESERVING OF THANKS as I put the final touches on this book. First, I want to thank my editor, David McNutt; marketing manager, Jeff Gissing; and the marvelous team at IVP Academic. You made this experience of publishing with IVP a real delight. Thank you so much for all of your insights, hard work, and precision. The book is stronger because of your collective wisdom.

Thanks to the trustees of Gordon-Conwell Theological Seminary for continuing to support faculty research and publication through a generous sabbatical program and to my preaching colleagues: Jeffrey Arthurs, Patricia Batten, and Pablo Jiménez for covering my teaching load and other responsibilities.

I could never thank my family enough for their continuous encouragement to engage in research and writing. Thank you Sarah, Ryan, Evan, and Aidan for giving me countless hours to pursue my calling of serving the church and the academy through publishing.

Thank you, Scott M. Gibson, for mentoring me. Your numerous kindnesses toward me and my family are completely undeserved. Thank you for encouraging me to preach and to teach homiletics. Thank you for believing in me and in God's calling on my life as a preacher and teacher when I felt discouraged. Thank you for spending time with me, discipling me, coaching me, and for sharing your life with me. Much of the wisdom in this book has been garnered from what you've taught me through apprenticeship. You've opened doors for me that I never envisioned. It's my joy and honor to dedicate this book to you. Thank you!

INTRODUCTION

■ ■ ■

I AM PERHAPS THE LAST PERSON to write a book on the topic of preaching for new and aspiring preachers. No, I am not just exaggerating as a feigned attempt at humility. Like a growing movement of seminarians, I sojourned to seminary during the summer of 1999 completely uncertain about what life after seminary would be like. In previous generations, most seminarians felt convinced of God's calling to the pastorate prior to taking the plunge of investing in a seminary education. However, I, as an extremely shy and introverted person, was not so sure if being a pastor was *my thing*. Like Moses in Exodus 4:13, I begged God often to use anyone but me.

During the first year of my MDiv program at Gordon-Conwell Theological Seminary, I quickly took to Greek and later became a research assistant for Aida Besançon Spencer, a New Testament professor. I daydreamed frequently about what life in the ivory tower would look like as a New Testament scholar. Soon any distant inklings for pastoral ministry began to dissolve. I started exploring doctoral programs in New Testament so that I would have a legitimate excuse not to serve as a full-time pastor and have to deal with the problems of others—let alone my worst fear which, God forbid, was standing in front of others to preach.

However, as I soon discovered, God has a sense of humor. I eventually took my first preaching class with the late Haddon W. Robinson, a masterful and renowned preacher, a luminary in the field of homiletics, and the author of the widely used textbook *Biblical Preaching*. In the first class he shared, "There are two types of preachers. One preacher speaks for twenty minutes, but it feels like an hour. The other preacher speaks for an hour, but it feels like twenty minutes. My life's journey has been trying to figure out what makes the difference." In that moment, God stirred in me an initial interest in preaching. I too, like Robinson, wanted to know what the difference was. Yet in my sermon for his class, I completely blanked and burned in the middle of the message. For the sake of clarity and simplicity, Robinson believed in and championed a no-notes policy, and I obviously needed them in that moment. I felt like a third category of preacher that Robinson had not even mentioned—an utter preaching failure.

Moving on to my second preaching class, Scott M. Gibson graciously took me, a fragile young preacher, under his wing and began mentorship. I do not know why, but he shared how he sensed God's calling on my life to preach. I continued to work hard and took other preaching electives, and soon my love and passion for preaching ensued. After some time serving in the pastorate, I now teach preaching at Gordon-Conwell, by God's providence and grace. Each semester, I take immense satisfaction in encouraging, guiding, and nurturing novice preachers. How far God has taken me on this journey! How much more I long to improve as his messenger! For those whom God calls to preach, God will work in and through us for his glory.

I am writing this book, first, because I believe in preaching. In his classic volume *Preaching and Preachers*, D. Martyn Lloyd-Jones writes, "The work of preaching is the highest and the greatest and most glorious calling to which anyone can ever be called."[1] Throughout history, God has transformed lives through Christian proclamation. God believes in preaching. He has often spoken into my life through sermons as well as touching the lives of millions who have cared to listen to them. Second, I believe in you—God's preachers—both beginning and seasoned ones. You are the very "jars of clay" about whom the apostle Paul writes in 2 Corinthians 4:7 who carry and impart the "treasure" of this good news. Third, I love and cherish God's people in the local church who are the valuable recipients of the preached Word.

Whether you have yet to preach your first sermon or you have preached scores of messages, I have written this book with you in mind. You may be a student in Bible college or seminary, a pastor, parachurch worker, lay leader in your congregation, professor of preaching hoping to inspire more students, or simply someone who is interested in preaching. Regardless of your station in life, you have picked up this Little Book because you want to develop in your preaching. My prayer is that this book will ignite a fire in you to preach God's Word with great passion, courage, love, faith, and care.

The book in your hands is not a homiletics textbook per se, although it may serve as one for some preachers in training. There are fine comprehensive resources available for the nuts and

---

[1] D. Martyn Lloyd-Jones, *Preaching and Preachers* (Grand Rapids: Zondervan, 1971), 9.

bolts of putting together a sermon.[2] Instead, this book is more accurately a primer or introduction to preaching focusing on the characteristics of what makes for effective sermons and faithful preachers. In part one, we will explore the question, Why study preaching? My hope is to inspire you toward or reignite your passion for preaching and why preaching matters. In part two, we will identify three central characteristics of faithful preaching: interpretation of Scripture, cultural exegesis, and application. Finally, in part three, we will explore three foundational qualities of faithful preachers: being loving, being a person of integrity, and being prayerful.

To be clear, I am a fellow adventurer and learner just like you in this thing called preaching. By no means do I write this book because I have arrived as a preacher—far from it. In fact, no preacher should ever think that he or she has *arrived*. Rather, I have simply sat where you sit and have stood where you stand. I have preached hundreds of sermons and also worked with hundreds of beginning as well as experienced preachers. And I want to share with you some of the things I have learned along the way

---

[2]See, for example, Bryan Chapell, *Christ-Centered Preaching: Redeeming the Expository Sermon*, 3rd ed. (Grand Rapids: Baker Academic, 2018); Terry G. Carter and J. Scott Duvall, *Preaching God's Word: A Hands-On Approach to Preparing, Developing, and Delivering the Sermon*, 2nd ed. (Grand Rapids: Zondervan, 2018); Timothy Keller, *Preaching: Communicating Faith in an Age of Skepticism* (New York: Viking, 2015); Abraham Kuruvilla, *A Manual for Preaching: The Journey from Text to Sermon* (Grand Rapids: Baker Academic, 2019); Haddon W. Robinson, *Biblical Preaching: The Development and Delivery of Expository Messages*, 3rd ed. (Grand Rapids: Baker Academic, 2014); and Ramesh Richard, *Preparing Expository Sermons: A Seven-Step Method for Biblical Preaching* (Grand Rapids: Baker, 2001).

about preaching and preachers—including what we might do and even a few things to avoid.

Furthermore, my desire here is to embolden you regarding the challenges and opportunities afforded to us as preachers of God's Word. By the end of this book, my hope and prayer for you is twofold: that your reservations about preaching and being a preacher will be mitigated and that your interest in and even enthusiasm for preaching will be kindled. As the apostle Paul wrote to Timothy, "Preach the word; be prepared in season and out of season; correct, rebuke and encourage—with great patience and careful instruction" (2 Tim 4:2). Thanks for joining me as we prepare for this great and glorious calling—to be preachers of the living Word of God! Can you believe that he uses even *us*?

PART ONE

WHY STUDY PREACHING?

1

PREACHING

The Forgotten Discipline

■■■

MUSIC ICON MADONNA VERBALIZED the culture's sentiment toward preaching when she sang the indelible lyrics "Papa don't preach!" in her 1986 *True Blue* album. British homiletician Jolyon Mitchell observes: "Madonna's hit song *Papa Don't Preach* shows how the verb 'preach' often now reverberates with negative associations. The words 'preach' and 'preaching' have come to mean 'to give unwelcome or unnecessary moral or religious advice.'"[1] Madonna and Mitchell were ahead of the curve in understanding our post-Christian culture. Preaching has fallen on hard times. First, society and culture at large do not seem to have high esteem for preaching. Such pejorative attitudes toward preaching have only exacerbated the problem in the years ensuing. Skeptics have an allergy or even an aversion to the very word *preaching*.

Second, the title of this opening chapter reflects how preaching often is not highly regarded in theological education. I can still feel the jolt of patronizing jabs during my doctoral

---

[1]Jolyon P. Mitchell, *Visually Speaking: Radio and the Renaissance of Preaching* (Louisville: Westminster/John Knox, 1999), 13.

studies at the University of Edinburgh. Fellow students would hear "I'm doing a PhD in homiletics" and snidely ask, "Is that really an academic discipline?" Whether in the United Kingdom, United States, or elsewhere, an illusory hierarchy permeates across theological education. Biblical scholars represent a top tier or upper echelon of seminary academicians. They do "real research." Biblical and systematic theologians also represent esteemed theological educators whose work is taken seriously.

Practical theologians, however, like homileticians, counselors, Christian educators, Christian ethicists, and others fall under their own lowly classification, and their disciplines are becoming forgotten in seminary. A homiletician who teaches in the divinity school of a well-known research university once shared with me how homileticians' offices resided in the basement of the office building because "sermonizers" were kept separate from the rest of the school's faculty.

In light of such disparaging times, some seminaries are capitulating to the culture and even decreasing their preaching course requirements. I have witnessed that a growing number of seminarians are not taking their preaching classes seriously and their institutions are increasingly requiring only one preaching class, thus giving the appearance that it is not that difficult or significant. Sometimes professors who teach the Bible and theology make snarky comments directly or indirectly about preaching and practical ministry courses as being inferior subjects. A common unspoken attitude is that "anyone can teach preaching."[2]

---

[2]Scott M. Gibson, "The Place of Preaching Professors in Theological Education," in *Training Preachers: A Guide to Teaching Homiletics*, ed. Scott M. Gibson (Bellingham, WA: Lexham, 2018), 21.

Third, even in certain church contexts, time for Scripture reading and the spoken Word have been reduced in the corporate worship service. Greater worship time is allocated for announcements, singing, liturgies, testimonies, interviews, dramas and skits, multimedia, and other elements of worship. The traditional sermon seems increasingly antiquated in our ADHD, media-saturated church culture. Listeners' limited attention spans have resulted in shrinking time for the sermon. As Lori Carrell observes, "To many pastors, it doesn't look like the church honors the centrality of preaching. It's a system that can keep pastors from knowing that preaching matters."[3]

Curbing these attitudinal trends, I want to make a case in this opening chapter for the importance of preaching in theological education and in the life of the church. The spoken Word remains a critical component to congregational vitality. However, exegetically sloppy, underprepared, and applicationally irrelevant sermons have produced a spiritual malaise across many North American congregations and abroad. At the same time, preaching is often a polarizing discipline, which either excites or petrifies preachers. Since I have gone through my share of struggles and identity crises as a preacher and teacher of preachers, I want to encourage seminarians, new pastors, and experienced ones as they consider their calling to preach and to inject them with a vision for effectively preaching God's Word—and why that matters. I will begin by addressing two common fears that potential preachers and even veteran communicators associate with the task of preaching.

---

[3]Bob Wells, "Congregant Feedback Can Improve Pastors' Sermons, SPE Study Finds," accessed March 22, 2018, www.faithandleadership.com /programs/spe/articles/200806/feedback.html.

THE FEAR OF PUBLIC SPEAKING

Standing in front of others to communicate—in any context—is a deep-seated fear in our society. Speech anxiety or *glossophobia* literally means "tongue" and "fear or dread" and is the phobia of speaking or speaking in public.[4] Surveys suggest that approximately 75 percent of all people experience this fear, which means we fear speaking in public more than we even fear death.[5]

Why do we fear public speaking so much? Much of glossophobia stems from our own feelings of inadequacy. Here are six common insecurities of preachers and communicators.

Knowledge. Perhaps we are afraid to expose our lack of knowledge about a given subject or about the Bible. We may also fear people's pushback and wonder if we have the intellectual chops to respond intelligently to their questions and challenges.

Appearance. We might be anxious about what we look like in front of others and their perceptions about our physical appearance, skin color and countenance (especially for ethnic minorities), birthmarks, hair color and hair styles, clothing and fashion sense, accessories, height, weight, and the like.

Voice. People often dislike the timbre or tone of their own speaking voice. We wish that we could all sound like Hollywood actors such as Morgan Freeman, Meryl Streep, and James Earl Jones or well-known preachers like Joel Gregory, Barbara Brown

---

[4]Adam McClafferty, "12 'Fear of Public Speaking' Symptoms and How to Beat Them," *Forbes*, January 12, 2015, www.forbes.com/sites/alex mcclafferty/2015/01/12/fear-of-public-speaking/#14d22d393ca1.

[5]Glenn Croston, "The Thing We Fear More Than Death: Why Predators Are Responsible for Our Fear of Public Speaking," *Psychology Today*, November 29, 2012, www.psychologytoday.com/blog/the-real-story-risk /201211/the-thing-we-fear-more-death.

Taylor, and the late Haddon Robinson, whose rich voices made for excellent radio or television broadcasting.

Forgetfulness. Perhaps we are terrified that we will forget what we are going to say and stare blankly into the crowd with unspeakable shame. Forgetting our sermon causes particularly acute anxiety for those who use no notes or minimal notes in the pulpit.

Rejection. Some fear that our communication or inability to communicate will lead to a form of rejection—whether it is the rejection of our ideas or the outright rejection of our personhood. We do not want to be told directly or behind our backs that we are boring, uninteresting, confusing, lacking creativity, and more.

Past experience. We might fear the replication of demoralizing past experiences in school and other social settings such as speaking in front of others at science fairs, debate clubs, student government, poetry slams, church Sunday school classes, and other life moments where we experienced humiliation in some way. Maybe you vowed never to put yourself in situations to relive such torture again.

Over the years, I have had a number of seminary students tell me that they switched degree programs because they dreaded taking our two required preaching courses at Gordon-Conwell Theological Seminary. The fear of public speaking forces many to prematurely abandon a preaching ministry in order to pursue ministry positions that are less public and more behind-the-scenes.

TAKING CRITICISM PERSONALLY

For most if not all preachers, feelings about our preaching bear resemblance to our feelings about our child. We crave affirmation and thrive on the praises of others about the positive

characteristics of our offspring, such as her beautiful countenance, intelligence, creativity, and musical or athletic abilities.
However, we despise anyone who dares to utter anything negative about our child—that she is somehow deficient or fails to
measure up. Just as children are a direct reflection of Mom and
Dad, sermons are our homiletical babies and reflect the preacher.
Congregants leaving the worship sanctuary on Sunday morning
conjure up a nice parting phrase for the preacher whether the
sermon hit home or not. At least, many pastors feel that way.

Constructive comments are difficult to hear, especially when
it comes to our sermons. Now that I make a living by telling
students the strengths and weaknesses of their preaching, I find
myself reliving the first sermons I ever preached. Even as a novice
preacher, fumbling and bumbling my way to write down something sermon-esque, I still found it excruciating to hear anything
constructive about my preaching. Just ask my wife! We had fre-
quent spats during the car ride home from Sunday services due
to my insecurity and incessant need to fish for compliments. But
it is a true blessing to have trusted people who can speak the
truth into our lives. Like anything, we rarely become better at a
particular skill without receiving constructive criticism.

The struggle is that many beginners think that they are innately good preachers—I am thinking here of my novice
preaching students. A neophyte golfer would never see himself
or herself as being a pro, especially after exhausting eighteen
strokes on the very first hole, but preachers are a different species.
When it comes to our preaching, our egos cannot handle the
criticism. For this reason, I try to be extra gracious in my word
choice when I evaluate students' sermons.

The fear of criticism in preaching can lead to several responses. First, we may choose to preserve our dignity and cling to our self-importance so we leave the pulpit in favor of other types of ministry positions. Second, we can get defensive about our preaching and dismiss others' viewpoints. Third, we only ask for feedback from people who respond well to our sermons. Think of the doting grandmother or grandfather type in the second pew. But, fourth, we can listen to and grow from constructive comments, recognizing that they are not personal attacks but rather encouragements to improve our homiletical craftsmanship.

I tell my preaching students to start pinching themselves on the wrist from day one. To learn how to preach effectively requires thick skin. If we allow ourselves to ride the homiletical roller coaster every Sunday in experiencing the highs and lows based on listeners' praiseworthy or critical comments, our preaching ministry will fizzle out quickly. We will ultimately give less glory to God even though we believe our preaching is an act of obedience. Constructive criticism comes with the preaching territory. We cannot take ourselves and others' remarks too seriously. We remind ourselves that we are preaching for an audience of one. Indeed, God's people matter, but every time we stand to preach, we desire to faithfully and lovingly deliver God's message because that is what *really* matters. Is my preaching faithful to God?

While preaching seemingly takes a back seat in society, the academy, and sometimes even in the church, I want to suggest a few reasons why the study of preaching matters. The following perspectives aim to shed some light on its significance for the church.

Good Preaching Is Valued and Necessary

People in the pews still value good, biblical preaching. According to Lydia Saad in a Gallup survey, one of the most important factors for why churchgoers attend a particular church is the preaching, more specifically, the desire to hear "sermons relevant to life (75%)" and "sermons teaching Scripture (76%)."[6] A study at the Center for Excellence in Congregational Leadership reveals strongly, according to Bob Wells, that "preaching matters deeply to listeners."[7] Kenneth Carder at Duke Divinity School observes that "the three qualities that congregations . . . most commonly wanted in a new pastor were *love and care for people, understanding of commitment to the Gospel*, and *strong preaching*."[8]

Preachers can take heart because people in the pews still hunger for faithful exposition of Scripture. Just as orphans starve for physical food and do not even realize that they are malnourished, God's people are similarly famished and yearn to be nourished with the whole counsel of God. They want to know how the Bible connects and speaks to their daily lives—their joys, sorrows, questions, and concerns. Preachers have the privilege of serving the church as spiritual dieticians. Preaching God's truth faithfully week by week enables us to feed our sheep a balanced diet to nurture them in their process of sanctification.

---

[6]Lydia Saad, "Sermon Content Is What Appeals Most to Churchgoers," Gallup, April 14, 2017, www.gallup.com/poll/208529/sermon-content -appeals-churchgoers.aspx.

[7]Wells, "Congregant Feedback."

[8]Kenneth L. Carder, "Preaching Matters for Pastoral Excellence," accessed June 26, 2019, www.faithandleadership.com/programs/spe/articles/200806 /matters.html.

> The three qualities that congregations . . . most commonly wanted in a new pastor were *love and care for people, understanding of commitment to the Gospel*, and *strong preaching*.
>
> Kenneth Carder,
> "Preaching Matters for Pastoral Excellence"

PREACHING IS AN ACT OF LEADERSHIP

Second, preaching is a vital tool for leadership. Leadership is *the* buzzword in the business world, just as it has become one in the church today.[9] We often synthesize pastoral ministry with leadership and even use the word *pastor* synonymously with *leader*. Preaching is not just giving a talk, sharing a message, or giving a lecture. I am sure we have heard those comments before. Rather, it is a manifestation and extension of our leadership and a central exercise for leading and casting vision for our congregation. Kenton Anderson says, "Preaching is leadership. Preachers who resist their role as leaders are doing something less than what preaching is."[10]

---

[9]Scores of books are published each year by major Christian publishers on pastoral leadership, such as Aubrey Malphurs, *Developing Emotionally Mature Leaders: How Emotional Intelligence Can Help Transform Your Ministry* (Grand Rapids: Baker Books, 2018); Larry Osborne, *Lead Like a Shepherd: The Secret to Leading Well* (Nashville: Thomas Nelson, 2018); Tod Bolsinger, *Canoeing the Mountains: Christian Leadership in Uncharted Territory* (Downers Grove, IL: InterVarsity Press, 2018); Tara Beth Leach, *Emboldened: A Vision for Empowering Women in Ministry* (Downers Grove, IL: InterVarsity Press, 2017); Nicole Massie Martin, *Made to Lead: Empowering Women for Ministry* (St. Louis: Chalice, 2016); and Mandy Smith, *The Vulnerable Pastor: How Human Limitations Empower Our Ministry* (Downers Grove, IL: InterVarsity Press, 2015).

[10]See Kenton Anderson, "Preaching as Leadership," July 19, 2017, www.integrativepreaching.wordpress.com/2017/07/19/preaching-as-leadership/.

In basic terms, leadership is having influence in the lives of others. The ability to lead a congregation well through one's preaching ministry is a powerful medium for communicating and casting vision, voicing words of encouragement and disseminating hope, sharing sympathy and empathy, infusing energy and vitality, and more.

One way to view the task of preaching is casting vision, what we might call *dream casting*. In every sermon, one of my intentional goals is to help my listeners cast new dreams for their lives, which align with the sermon's text.[11] We might challenge our hearers by asking them questions like, "What would your life look like in Christ if you weren't preoccupied with the things of this world such as, fear, comfort, gadgets, appearance, reputation, body image, 401Ks, name brands, job promotions, titles, accolades, children's success, and more?" We all have certain idols and vices that keep us hovering over the line between our Christian future and pre-Christian past. Each sermon provides an opportunity to invite listeners and provide space to dream new spiritual dreams.

Preaching elicits great dreaming for God. Therefore, your sermon matters. As God reminds the prophet Isaiah, "It [my Word] will not return to me empty, but will accomplish what I desire and achieve the purpose for which I sent it" (Is 55:11). Preaching equips the saints for a God-given vision for what their days, weeks, months, and years will look like as they passionately

---

[11]Another fruitful sociological concept is helping your listeners create spiritual "possible selves" for their lives. See Matthew D. Kim, *Preaching to Second Generation Korean Americans: Towards a Possible Selves Contextual Homiletic* (New York: Peter Lang, 2007), 129-60; and Kim, *Preaching with Cultural Intelligence* (Grand Rapids: Baker Academic, 2017), 21-22.

live out the Scriptures that you, the preacher, have exposited and unveiled for them. Preaching is not something we do simply because Christian tradition expects a word from the pastor or because it's a routine part of our worship service. We preach because God has something to say to his people—a message that often counteracts culture and galvanizes loving obedience to his instructions. We preach to lead our congregations in living out kingdom values in a messy world chock-full of griefs and anxieties. We preach in order to lead God's people because preaching is a pathway for leadership.

PREACHING IS THE CAPSTONE OF BIBLICAL STUDIES AND THEOLOGY

Finally, preaching is the very cross section and consummation of all other theological disciplines. Effective biblical preaching combines a depth of understanding regarding biblical exegesis, biblical theology, systematic theology, church history, counseling, sociology, psychology, anthropology, cultural exegesis, and all other disciplines in a seminary education. Preaching should not be the forgotten discipline of seminary. In fact, Swiss practical theologians like Bernard Reymond argue, "Homiletics is not a peripheral discipline, but a *central*, even *focal*, discipline of theology."[12] Preaching is where we find the wisdom of God. As Paul writes to the Corinthian believers, "For since in the wisdom of God the world through its wisdom did not know him, God was pleased through the foolishness of what was preached to

---

[12]Bernard Reymond, "Homiletics and Theology: Re-evaluating Their Relationship," in *The Modern Churchman* New Series XXXIV, no. 5 (1993), 38.

save those who believe" (1 Cor 1:21). God has not given up on preaching, and neither should we!

> Homiletics is not a peripheral discipline, but a *central*, even *focal*, discipline of theology.
>
> Bernard Reymond, "Homiletics and Theology"

CONCLUSION

Preaching matters because preaching is about God and his plan for the world. As Mary Hulst observes, "In fact, our sermons should do more than just *mention* God. They should be all about God: who God is, what he has done, what he is doing, what he will do. When we speak about God, our words should create in our hearers a deeper desire to know and love God more."[13] We also preach because God uses the vehicle of preaching to transform peoples' lives. Preaching is God's choice medium in gathered worship to bring vision, unity, and purpose to our lives as we see how we can participate in God's kingdom work. Proclamation from the pulpit is our weekly opportunity to present the gospel clearly and to make plain what Christlikeness looks like. For this reason, we want to become more effective preachers and to make every sermon count. We have inherited a great legacy in the act of preaching and that legacy needs to continue.

---

[13]Mary S. Hulst, *A Little Handbook for Preachers: Ten Practical Ways to a Better Sermon by Sunday* (Downers Grove, IL: InterVarsity Press, 2016), 34, italics original.

2

PREACHING

A Great Legacy

■ ■ ■

"I HAVE LONG LOOKED UPON PREACHING, and graciously experienced it, as a burdensome joy,"[1] observes James Earl Massey, a legendary African American preacher. Representing God as his messenger comes with a great weight and responsibility. You might feel the burden of preaching every time you stand up to preach in the form of sweat, stomachaches, nervousness, butterflies, headaches, a pulsating heart, and other physical manifestations. On the other hand, maybe you feel like Eric Liddell in the movie *Chariots of Fire* and only feel God's pleasure when preaching.

Whatever our particular response may be, the question for us is this: Why do we preach? Why do we spend hundreds of hours in sermon preparation every year? This chapter reminds us of the significant legacy that preaching holds in the life of the church. I begin by acknowledging some reasons why preaching can feel like a burdensome calling. Next, I offer rationales for why rightly

---

[1]James Earl Massey, *The Burdensome Joy of Preaching* (Nashville: Abingdon, 1998), 13.

motivated preaching produces joy and celebration. Last, I consider examples from Scripture and church history, which demonstrate the great legacy of preaching and why the preaching of the Word will endure in the lives of God's worshipers.

A GREAT BURDEN

It is mind-blowing to think that mere mortals can speak on behalf of the God of the universe. Throughout history, legends of the faith have shuddered, stammered, and resisted the calling to serve as God's mouthpiece to God's people. In the past and present, there are unnecessary burdens we can shoulder in the calling and task of preaching.

The burden of the self. Moses was one of the best-known figures in the Bible to question God's call to preach—in this case, to communicate with Pharaoh in order to liberate the Israelites from slavery. Moses responds to God in Exodus 3:11, "Who am I that I should go to Pharaoh and bring the Israelites out of Egypt?" Humans innately find faults in themselves, in our God-given abilities, and even in God's calling. We can get in our own way (making various excuses as Moses did) and try to obstruct the will of God and reject the privilege of being used by him.

If we are honest, we either mourn our deficiencies or we succumb to "abilititis," a hyper-reliance on one's gifts and thinking we can preach effectively by personal strengths and competencies.[2] Edwin H. Byington recalls a preacher whose ministry was curtailed because "the man's career had been

---

[2]Edwin H. Byington, *Pulpit Mirrors* (New York: George H. Doran, 1927), 28. Thanks to Scott M. Gibson for this insight.

spoiled by his great natural talents. . . . The fact is that abilititis, the excessive reliance on natural abilities and their abnormal development, is a common and dangerous homiletical disease."[3] It often produces lazy, ineffective, and uncircumspect preachers.

The burden of time. Stopping time is impossible. But deciding how we use and redeem that time is controllable. The vocation of pastor and preacher creates two types of responses to time management. Some take advantage of and abuse their freedom in the pastorate to be essentially indolent. However, I would prefer to give pastors the benefit of the doubt and suggest that many pastors struggle with the opposite extreme of being workaholics.

What can get wedged out of the pastoral workweek is space for sermon preparation. "Who has twelve to fifteen hours per week to prepare a Sunday message?" some might ask.[4] We can fall prey to laziness or distractions or perhaps being overly relational to the point that sermon preparation time gets nudged out. Even time or the misuse or misapplication of it can create undue homiletical burdens. We feel the relentless crunch of preaching as Haddon Robinson once put it, "Sundays roll around with amazing regularity—every three or four days!"[5]

The burden of comparison. Some pastors have quaked and cracked under the pressure of relentless preaching. Plagiarizing

---

[3]Byington, *Pulpit Mirrors*, 28-29.

[4]For example, see Ryan Huguley, *8 Hours or Less: Writing Faithful Sermons Faster* (Chicago: Moody, 2017).

[5]Jeffrey D. Arthurs, foreword to *Preaching Old Testament Narratives* by Benjamin H. Walton (Grand Rapids: Kregel, 2016), 17.

sermons is an epidemic across pulpits around the globe.[6] In our celebrity culture, pastors idolize "successful" pastors who headline preaching conferences and produce bestselling books with superhuman strength and regularity. It can be paralyzing to think that we can or must preach awe-inducing, inspirational, convicting, humorous, relatable, culturally sensitive, and easily applicable sermons every single week. However, we trust in the fact that we are simply God's messengers. As Alistair Begg encourages, "We gather together as the church not to enjoy preaching eloquence (or to criticize its lack) but to hear and heed the Word of God. We come to be exhorted, not entertained."[7]

Each generation of preachers has faced this gratuitous but very genuine burden of comparison, whether we label successful preachers as "communication kings or queens" or "celebrity pastors" whose pulpit personalities are larger than life.[8] Instead of thanking God for his or her good gifts and using them to the best of our ability, we easily become consumed with jealousy, envy, bitterness, or even animosity toward pastors who have seemingly received an inequitable "double portion" of communicative bliss and blessing from the Holy Spirit (2 Kings 2:9).

Each of these burdens of self, time, and comparison can be internalized by preachers, and they can cause our preaching to feel like an onerous, oppressive, even joyless task. However,

---

[6]See Scott M. Gibson, *Should We Use Someone Else's Sermon?: Preaching in a Cut-and-Paste World* (Grand Rapids: Zondervan, 2008).

[7]Alistair Begg, *Preaching for God's Glory* (Wheaton, IL: Crossway, 2010), 16.

[8]See Haddon W. Robinson, "Competing with the Communication Kings," in *Making a Difference in Preaching: Haddon Robinson on Biblical Preaching*, ed. Scott M. Gibson (Grand Rapids: Baker Books, 1998), 109-17.

when we intentionally focus on the great joy of preaching, and when we remember that God has called us to this task and leads us through the Spirit, these burdens can dissipate.

A GREAT JOY

Preaching, especially every Sunday, is taxing for any preacher. When preaching weekly for eight, twelve, or sixteen weeks straight or more, one can feel utterly depleted of any homiletical reserves. Our sermonic wooziness leaves us wanting to just get the sermon done. Yet when we deliberately center ourselves each week on God's Word and how God uses preaching, it rekindles great joy and slowly loosens lingering millstones. Scripture mentions at least three great joys that come from preaching.

The joy of the messenger. The apostle Paul understood the power and joyful pleasure of the preacher who obediently and faithfully proclaims the message of good news to the people to whom they are called. Paul writes in Romans 10:14-15, "How, then, can they call on the one they have not believed in? And how can they believe in the one of whom they have not heard? And how can they hear without someone preaching to them? And how can anyone preach unless they are sent? As it is written: 'How beautiful are the feet of those who bring good news!'" In his own mysterious way, God uses the proclamation of his Word to deliver the good news of salvation to all who hear it. We are privileged enough to be those very feet who transport this precious good news.

The joy of salvation and sanctification. Jesus says in Luke 15:7, "I tell you that in the same way there will be more rejoicing in heaven over one sinner who repents than over ninety-nine righteous persons who do not need to repent." The apostle Peter experienced heaven's joy of repentance exponentially in the aftermath of his sermon in Acts 2. As Luke records in Acts 2:37-38, "When the people heard this, they were cut to the heart and said to Peter and the other apostles, 'Brothers, what shall we do?' Peter replied, 'Repent and be baptized, every one of you, in the name of Jesus Christ for the forgiveness of your sins.'" Later in verse 41, it says, "Those who accepted his [Peter's] message were baptized, and about three thousand were added to their number that day."

Not only is witnessing initial saving faith thrilling, but also we are motivated by the visible transformation manifesting in our listeners' lives as they embody Romans 12:1-2 and become a "living sacrifice" for God. This same bountiful joy galvanizes twenty-first-century preachers as well. There's nothing like witnessing the Holy Spirit's miracle of a sinner's repentance that leads to salvation and heaven's rejoicing.

The joy of God's glory. God cares deeply about his glory. In fact, God wants to be glorified alone and will not share his glory with anyone or anything. As Isaiah 42:8 says, "I am the LORD; that is my name! I will not yield my glory to another or my praise to idols." God wants to be glorified in every sphere of life, including our proclamation. Peter says in 1 Peter 4:11, "If anyone speaks, they should do so as one who speaks the very words of God. If anyone serves, they should do so with the strength God provides, so that in all things God may be praised [also translated as *glorified*] through Jesus Christ. To him be the glory and the power for ever and ever. Amen."

What is your theology of preaching? Why do you preach? Sherwood Eliot Wirt observes, "Many people [including some preachers] do not understand the true purpose of a sermon. They think it is intended to be merely a Scripture lesson, a moral essay, a homily, an oration, a 'bit of uplift,' or even a socio-political discussion."[9] Rather, in preaching, we are concerned ultimately with the glory of God and drawing listeners closer to him. We preach because at the end of the day preaching is the business of exalting and glorifying God and not ourselves. We take no credit. There is no greater joy for the preacher than when God receives all of the glory, honor, and praise that he is rightfully due.

A Great Legacy

What do we leave our listeners each week in our preaching? Might our listeners miss something about our preaching once we are no longer in the pulpit? What is this great legacy that we have in the calling and task of preaching?[10]

Preaching has sat on a progressively steep precipice since the 1950s. W. E. Sangster, the great English Methodist minister, wrote in 1954, "Preaching is in the shadows. The world does not believe in it."[11] Fast-forward to the twenty-first century, where sermons

---

[9]Sherwood Eliot Wirt and Viola Blake, eds., *Great Preaching: Evangelical Messages by Contemporary Christians* (Waco, TX: Word Books, 1970), 11.

[10]See Zondervan's two-volume collection, *A Great Legacy: Apostles to the Revivalists*, vol. 1, ed. Benjamin K. Forrest, Kevin King Sr., William J. Curtis, and Dwayne Milioni (Grand Rapids: Zondervan, 2018) and *A Great Legacy: Enlightenment to the Present Day*, vol. 2, ed. Benjamin K. Forrest, Kevin King Sr., William J. Curtis, and Dwayne Milioni (Grand Rapids: Zondervan, 2018).

[11]W. E. Sangster, *The Craft of the Sermon* (Harrisburg, PA: Epworth Press, 1954), 1; see also Begg, *Preaching for God's Glory*, 13.

have often taken a back seat to interviews, question-and-answer sessions, testimonies, skits, movies, social media, and more. Two foundational questions we must ask are (1) Do we really believe in it? (2) Do we hold to a high view of preaching or not?

In contrast to the malaise, apathy, or even distain toward preaching that is happening in certain congregations, the luminary preacher John Stott once boldly said, "Preaching is indispensable to Christianity. Without preaching a necessary part of its authenticity has been lost. . . . We must speak what he has spoken. Hence the paramount obligation to preach."[12] He continues, "That preaching is central and distinctive to Christianity has been recognized throughout the Church's long and colourful story, even from the beginning."[13] We hold tightly to the great legacy of the proclamation of the good news of Jesus Christ.

The legacy of God's Word. The first great legacy is the legacy of God's eternal Word. Charles Swindoll writes starkly, "Do you realize there are only two eternal things on earth today? Only two: people and God's Word. Everything else will ultimately be burned up—*everything* else. Kind of sets your priorities straight, doesn't it?"[14] Quoting from Isaiah 40:8, the apostle Peter writes to the elders in 1 Peter 1:24-25 to assure them that: "For, 'All people are like grass, and all their glory is like the flowers of the field; the grass withers and the flowers fall, but the word of the Lord endures forever.' And this is the word that was preached to you."

---

[12]John Stott, *Between Two Worlds: The Challenge of Preaching Today*, (Grand Rapids: Eerdmans, 1982), 15.

[13]John Stott, *Between Two Worlds*, 16.

[14]Charles R. Swindoll, "What Lasts Forever? Only Two Things," July 8, 2015, www.insight.org/resources/article-library/individual/what-lasts-forever-only-two-things.

Scripture is God's great legacy to his people. In our increasingly biblically illiterate society, the Sunday sermon is perhaps the only time in a Christian's week where he or she actually reads the Bible and is taught God's Word. What a great legacy we are entrusted within teaching and preaching God's Word to God's people!

The legacy of heralds. In the history of the church, the greatest preachers knew their legacy and responsibility as heralds. The term herald (*kēryssein*) is not common or popular today. Yet as John Stott explains, "The herald has good news to proclaim to the whole world."[15] In other words, a herald is a proclaimer of God's truth demonstrated in the deity and person of Jesus Christ.[16] Heralds were not overly concerned with pulpit eloquence, with charisma, or with being liked and respected, but rather their chief motivation was to correctly *and* directly proclaim God's very Word in the Scriptures. Perhaps you have felt in recent decades the cultural shift away from heralding to simply being a charismatic and alluring "communicator" or "speaker" who can draw crowds.

A few examples from great preachers in history may help to solidify meaning in what a herald is and does. Augustine argues in his treatise *On Christian Doctrine* that the responsibility of preachers is to defend the Christian faith, to oppose error, and to instruct wisdom in the things that are right and to correct the

---

[15]John R. W. Stott, *The Preacher's Portrait: Some New Testament Word Studies* (Grand Rapids: Eerdmans, 1961), 33. Stott also uses here the images of steward, witness, father, and servant in addition to herald to describe the preacher.

[16]Robert Mounce, *The Essential Nature of New Testament Preaching* (Grand Rapids: Eerdmans, 1960), 52.

things that are wrong.[17] In part one of his *Religious Affections*, Jonathan Edwards states that Scripture is "opened, applied, and set home upon [people], in preaching."[18] Moreover, Charles Haddon Spurgeon, known as the "Prince of Preachers," wrote, "We insist upon it, that there must be abundance of matter in sermons, and next, that this matter must be congruous to the text . . . a real relationship between the sermon and its text."[19] Today, even centuries later, we also hold a great legacy of being the heralds, proclaimers, of God's Word to the world—a world that desperately needs to hear God's truth without mincing and altering its meaning.

> We insist upon it, that there must be abundance of matter in sermons, and next, that this matter must be congruous to the text . . . a real relationship between the sermon and its text.
>
> Charles Haddon Spurgeon, *Lectures to My Students*

The legacy of tradition. For some, tradition is synonymous with irrelevance, immutability, rigidness, antiquatedness, and other pejorative attributes. However, in a positive sense,

---

[17] Augustine, "On Christian Doctrine" 4.4.6, in *St. Augustine, City of God and Christian Doctrine*, vol. 2 of *Nicene and Post-Nicene Fathers of the Christian Church*, ed. Philip Schaff (Buffalo: Christian Literature, 1887), 576.

[18] Jonathan Edwards, "A Treatise Concerning Religious Affections," in *The Works of President Edwards*, vol. 3 (New York: Leavitt & Allen, 1857), 16.

[19] Charles Spurgeon, *Lectures to My Students* (Grand Rapids: Zondervan, 1954), 72.

tradition means preserving and celebrating the rich history, witness, and effect of previous generations of preachers and their preaching ministries. Reading up on the history of preaching can help us understand the great tradition of preaching: its challenges and joys, its preachers and the cultures to whom they preached.

The biographies and autobiographies of great preachers can provide modern preachers with a sense of comfort because even the greatest of preachers were imperfect, embodied various personality types (e.g., fiery, humorous, stoic, and others) and abilities (e.g., exegetical, charismatic, pastoral, applicable, and more), and held to various theological positions (e.g., dispensational, Reformed, Presbyterian, Baptist, Arminian, and Pentecostal, to name a few).[20] God has used preachers, even the most well-known and lauded, in spite of their inadequacies, sinful tendencies, and idiosyncrasies. For example, even though Charles Spurgeon is well-known for his preaching, he also was known to have struggled with depression.[21] We are all broken jars of clay, yet God has chosen to work through preachers.

It is helpful to remember that throughout the church's history the preaching of God's Word has taken place not within a vacuum but within a specific time and place.[22] Even so, the past shares many similarities with the present situation in our local churches. Warren Wiersbe observes,

---

[20]Warren W. Wiersbe, *The Dynamics of Preaching*, 3rd ed. (Grand Rapids: Baker Books, 2001), 143.

[21]See, for example, Zack Eswine, *Spurgeon's Sorrows: Realistic Hope for Those Who Suffer from Depression* (Fearn, Scotland: Christian Focus, 2014).

[22]Wiersbe, *The Dynamics of Preaching*, 144.

Each age in history has its own peculiar challenges, issues, and critical events, and seeing my preacher friends in their historical setting has helped me better understand why they thought, preached, and ministered as they did. . . . Younger preachers today may need to catch up on the past, and when they do, they'll discover how remarkably contemporary it is. There's nothing new under the sun or in the pulpit.[23]

The tradition of the church's preaching has been one of God's chosen vehicles to change lives. In his omniscience and omnipotence, God can employ any medium to draw his children closer to himself and to fulfill his kingdom's work. Yet one of the primary modes he has chosen to accomplish this work is that of preaching. Jonah preached against the wickedness of Nineveh and reluctantly offered a message of repentance (Jon 3:4). John the Baptist pointed to Jesus as the Lamb of God and preached, "Repent, for the kingdom of heaven has come near" (Mt 3:2). Jesus preached a countercultural message of what faith, love, and obedience looked like for new covenant people (Mt 5–7) that we can try to emulate. Peter preached an eschatological message of repentance, salvation, and the lordship of Christ (Acts 2:17-36). Paul's message in 1 Corinthians 2:2 summited ultimately in Christ: "For I resolved to know nothing while I was with you except Jesus Christ and him crucified."

The preaching tradition is not capricious or discretionary. Paul charged his young mentee, Timothy, in 2 Timothy 4:2, "Preach the word . . . in season and out of season." Preaching is a command, an imperative! It is not an optional feature in the

---

[23]Wiersbe, *The Dynamics of Preaching*, 144.

worship of God. It should not be easily discarded or hastily undertaken. Al Mohler writes, "Preaching is an inescapably theological act, for the preacher dares to speak of God and, in a very real sense, *for* God."[24] In his sovereign wisdom, God has decided upon preaching as an instrument to communicate his being, his character, his mission, his purpose, his will, his desires, his love, his holiness, his wrath, his Son, his Spirit, his pleasure, his displeasure, and all that he is and all that he has done for his people.

> Preach the word . . . in season and out of season.
>
> *2 Timothy 4:2*

CONCLUSION

Preaching is a part of our great tradition, established by God and enacted through human agents. Therefore, we do not undertake this charge lightly. It is God's great tradition. Although this task might at times feel like a burden, it is actually God's great legacy for us to enjoy and pass down from generation to generation. Moreover, this great legacy has a great mission: to make disciples.

---

[24]Albert Mohler, "Why Do We Preach? A Foundation for Christian Preaching, Part One," December 15, 2005, www.albertmohler.com/2005/12/15 /why-do-we-preach-a-foundation-for-christian-preaching-part-one/.

3

PREACHING

Making Disciples

■ ■ ■

IN NEARLY EVERY OCCUPATION, profession, or vocation, a person learns how to do a particular trade or skill with the big picture in view. Mechanics learn not just how to fix a carburetor or a muffler, but more importantly they learn how the entire car operates. Physicians do not train in medical school just to understand the ins and outs of how the kidneys or lungs function independently of each other. Rather, they learn about the entire anatomy and how every part of the human body functions as a unit. Preachers, similarly, do not preach a single sermon on a given passage or topic in isolation without attention to the larger task, a holistic understanding of how a lifetime of sermons work together to accomplish a transforming work in the lives of one's listeners.

In his Great Commission in Matthew 28:19-20, Jesus said, "Therefore go and make disciples of all nations, baptizing them in the name of the Father and of the Son and of the Holy Spirit, and teaching them to obey everything I have commanded you." Why do we preach? One of the ultimate purposes of preaching is to make disciples—sanctifying learners who love, obey, and serve God. In short, we preach to make disciples of Jesus Christ.

MOVING PREACHING TOWARD DISCIPLESHIP

What is a disciple? The simple definition of a disciple in Greek is *mathētēs*, a learner. A disciple learns from the master, and our master, teacher, Lord, and Savior is Jesus Christ. How do we learn as Christians? One primary way is through the preaching of the Word. David Schrock writes,

> Biblical discipleship begins with a biblical pulpit. . . . Because faith comes by hearing the gospel (Romans 10:17), Christ-centered, gospel-rich preaching is the starting point. For no matter how good a "discipleship program" a church has; its disciple-making won't rise above its preaching. Why? Because pastors are the lead exemplar for sharing the gospel, reading the Scripture, and applying the Bible to all of life.[1]

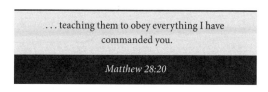

> . . . teaching them to obey everything I have commanded you.
>
> *Matthew 28:20*

While preaching *alone* does not produce disciples or reinforce discipleship, a steady, weekly, intentional diet of messages will build, edify, and guide a congregation toward greater discipleship. Scott M. Gibson communicates the important relationship between preaching and discipleship. Gibson says, "Preaching is discipleship."[2] How do we preach with discipleship

---

[1]David Schrock, "How Preaching Makes Disciples," Southern Equip, accessed June 26, 2019, equip.sbts.edu/article/what-has-preaching-to-do -with-discipleship/.

[2]Scott M. Gibson, *Preaching with a Plan: Sermon Strategies for Growing Mature Believers* (Grand Rapids: Baker Books, 2012), 14, 17.

in view? In addition, what effect does preaching as discipleship have on the lives of our listeners?

PREACHING AS DISCIPLESHIP LEADS TO OBEDIENCE

Many preachers and missionaries focus on the *going* part of the Great Commission and perhaps even the importance of baptizing new converts. Of course, these are essential elements in the disciple-making process. What often gets overlooked, however, is the latter part where Jesus says, "Teaching them to obey everything I have commanded you." If we are honest, we live in a culture that is obedience averse. When God says go, we like to stay. We do not like to hear the words *obey* and *obedience,* nor do we want to live them out. That includes pastors and preachers.

Therefore, the first and primary question we need to ask is introspective: How are we doing as preachers in our obedience to the Word? Ed Stetzer writes, "I believe that we would see more fruitful discipleship in our churches if we were to start by questioning our own spiritual formation before we question the development of those we lead and disciple."[3] The Bible is replete with examples of what it means to obey God in every area of our lives: for example, the Decalogue (Ex 20 and Deut 5), Jesus' Sermon on the Mount (Matt 5–7), and Paul's affirmation of the fruit of the Spirit (Gal 5:22-23). In our age of compartmentalization, we may fail to address our personal obedience, forgetting

---

[3]Ed Stetzer, foreword to *Rediscovering Discipleship: Making Jesus' Final Words Our First Work* by Robby Gallaty (Grand Rapids: Zondervan, 2015), 11.

that we are Christians and disciples first before we are pastors and preachers.

Some Christians may ask, Why does God call for obedience, and why should our sermons emphasize obedience? Doesn't it promote moralism when the preacher hollers, "Stop drinking, smoking, swearing, working so much, neglecting your family, dancing, lusting, slandering, spending, and gossiping"? In many sermons, behavior modification is the intended or unintended goal, which can lead to moralism. Moralistic preaching demands behavioral change and morality without a proper grounding in the gospel. It calls the listener to do more, be more, stop more, give more, and serve more simply as ends in themselves without the theology and Spirit-led power to accomplish this work. Matt Woodley defines it this way: "Moralistic preaching is leaving people alone in their sin, leaving people alone in their challenge, without surrounding them with the grace of God the Father, the power of the risen Christ, and the power of the Holy Spirit."[4]

In a skit on the comedy series *Mad TV*, actor Bob Newhart plays the character of a psychologist who in one of the episodes offers sage advice to a woman struggling with the fear of getting buried alive. Newhart builds up the moment and eventually offers two words of wisdom: "Stop it!" She incredulously inquires, "Stop it?" Newhart confirms, "Yes, S-T-O-P, new word, I-T."[5] Moralistic preaching in many ways is a version of "stop it" preaching.

---

[4]Matt Woodley, "Why and How to Avoid Moralistic Preaching," November 14, 2017, in *Preaching Today: Monday Morning Preacher*, podcast, 13:20, www.preachingtoday.com/media/podcast/why-and-how-to-avoid -moralistic-preaching.html.

[5]*Mad TV*, season 6, episode 24, featuring Bob Newhart, aired May 12, 2001, on Fox Network.

We simply reiterate "stop it" in moralistic sermons guised using various Scripture verses.[6]

Throughout Scripture, God requires obedience from his people. For instance, the Hebrew verb for *obey* (*šāmaʿ*), which means "to hear, listen, pay attention to, perceive, obey, proclaim, announce," is used 1,165 times and its cognate (*šāmar*) meaning "to keep" is used 468 times.[7] In the New Testament, the Greek verb for *obey* (*tēreō*), "to keep, obey; guard, protect," is used seventy times, while *hypakouō*, rendered "to obey, do what one is told to do," is used twenty-one times.[8] God doesn't take the subject of obedience lightly. Nor does Jesus decrease the significance of obedience in the gospels. Jesus says in John 14:15, "If you love me, keep [or obey] my commands." In other words, our love for Jesus can be measured by whether or not we keep or obey his commands. Preaching as discipleship leads to obedience. As we teach people to obey God's Word, we must also help them to see "why and how" to follow God's Word.[9]

PREACHING AS DISCIPLESHIP
LEADS TO CHRISTLIKENESS

As we disciple others through our preaching, God's Word leads believers to Christlikeness. Paul writes to the church in Colossae,

---

[6]Similarly, legalistic preaching makes the Christian life simply about following a bunch of rules and regulations. It is preaching law without grace. Both forms of preaching are anthropomorphic, focusing on people, their sins and limitations, and their efforts to improve without acknowledging that gospel transformation comes through the work of Jesus Christ through the power of the Holy Spirit.

[7]William D. Mounce, *Mounce's Complete Expository Dictionary of Old and New Testament Words* (Grand Rapids: Zondervan, 2006), 477.

[8]Mounce, *Mounce's Complete Expository Dictionary*, 477.

[9]Woodley, "Why and How to Avoid."

"He [Jesus Christ] is the one we proclaim, admonishing and teaching everyone with all wisdom, so that we may present everyone fully mature in Christ" (Col 1:28).[10] In our preaching and teaching, our goal is to "present everyone fully mature [complete] in Christ." That means week by week, season by season, year by year, our listeners should look more like Christ in every area of their lives. Our role as preachers is to guide them in this process of sanctification.

In our post-Christian society, we are in a constant battle of nonconformity to the image of Christ. It is not in our human nature to desire Christlikeness. Rather, we fall back on Christ's grace and ask for leniency and even validation of *our* dreams and desires. The story goes that President Abraham Lincoln was once attending a prayer breakfast when he was encouraged by one minister to pray that God would be on our side. President Lincoln nuanced the prayer differently, responding that we should pray that we are on God's side. Just as Jesus said to his Father, "Not my will, but yours be done," so also the Christian seeks to live out God's will and not our own.

With an inauthentic hyper-reliance on God's grace, much preaching today fails to lead listeners toward Christlikeness. We have become a generation of people-pleasing preachers tolerating sin whether silently or, even worse, vocally. Christians today often ask preachers the wrong questions. Rather than asking God about how to be more Christlike, we ask how much sin he is willing to forgive after the fact. Instead, faithful preaching can reveal our failings, point us to the grace of God found in Christ, and encourage genuine discipleship.

---

[10]See also Kim, *Preaching with Cultural Intelligence* (Grand Rapids: Baker Academic, 2017), 4.

PREACHING AS DISCIPLESHIP
CHANGES WHAT WE LOVE

Preaching with a view toward discipleship changes what we love. In my experience, few people actually enjoy eating healthy foods from a young age. Rather, through repetition, we can modify our palates to the point of voluntarily selecting the healthy over the harmful. The sermon is a central vehicle for advancing discipleship through changing our earthly and spiritual palates. James K. A. Smith writes,

> Discipleship, we might say, is a way to curate your heart, to be attentive to and intentional about what you love. So discipleship is more a matter of hungering and thirsting than of knowing and believing. Jesus's command to follow him (Mt 16:24) is a command to align our loves and longings with his—to want what God wants, to desire what God desires, to hunger and thirst after God and crave a world where he is all in all—a vision encapsulated by the shorthand "the kingdom of God."[11]

In our sermons, we can help our listeners change what they love. Yes, but how? Obviously, this is not a simple fix. However, the message, no matter how difficult the content, is received better when one understands that God's commands for us are preceded by God's love for us. For instance, Jeffrey Arthurs explains that in our preaching we are more effective when we ground "the imperative in the indicative" demonstrating a causal relationship

---

[11]James K. A. Smith, *You Are What You Love: The Spiritual Power of Habit* (Grand Rapids: Brazos, 2016), 2.

such as in 1 John 4:11, where it says, "Dear friends, since God so loved us, we also ought to love one another."[12]

> Discipleship is more a matter of hungering and thirsting than of knowing and believing.
>
> James K. A. Smith, *You Are What You Love*

Yet this relationship between the indicative and imperative is not limited to epistles alone. As an example, God says to the assembly in Leviticus 19:2, "Be holy because I, the LORD your God, am holy." We are commanded to holiness (imperative). Why? Because God is holy (indicative). When our listeners understand the reason for the demand, it becomes easier to understand why the imperative is necessary. As our love and affection for God grows, we desire to be like him. Authority lies in God's Word, which means we are not the authority even though so often we would like to be.[13]

Thankfully, we are not alone in this enterprise of transformation: "God has not left us at the mercy of our desires. He offers us hope in reminding us that our desires are cultivated and not immutable. And because the Holy Spirit dwells within us, we can trust that he will change our affections toward Christ for the glory of God."[14] Preaching as discipleship changes what we love.

---

[12]Jeffrey D. Arthurs, *Preaching with Variety: How to Re-create the Dynamics of Biblical Genres* (Grand Rapids: Kregel, 2007), 155-56.

[13]Donald R. Sunukjian, *Invitation to Biblical Preaching: Proclaiming Truth with Clarity and Relevance* (Grand Rapids: Kregel, 2007), 9.

[14]Ethics and Religious Liberty Commission of the Southern Baptist Convention, "How Our Affections Follow Our Actions," November 25, 2014, www.erlc.com/resource-library/articles/how-our-affections-follow-our-actions.

Again, I'm not imploring you to preach moralistic sermons. We cannot possibly change ourselves apart from Christ and the power of the Holy Spirit. Rather, we preach because our preaching seeks to increase discipleship, and a significant part of that discipleship process is loving God through our obedience, becoming more Christlike, and changing what we love.

CONCLUSION

In this first part (chapters one through three), we have considered some reasons for why we preach and why preaching is significant for the life of the church. Preaching is part of a great and lasting legacy of making disciples of Jesus Christ. It is not the forgettable or dispensable discipline of seminary or the church. Preaching is essential to the life of God's people because understanding and applying the Word of God is essential. In part two, we will shift our focus to identify three central characteristics of what makes for faithful preaching.

PART TWO

CHARACTERISTICS OF
FAITHFUL PREACHING

4

FAITHFUL INTERPRETATION

■ ■ ■

EVERY NIGHT, I TRY TO READ a section of Scripture with my sons before they go to sleep. One of them will take a turn to read a few verses, and then we discuss it together. When children read Scripture, they are not simply sounding out difficult names and words phonetically, like *Mephibosheth* or *Sadducees*. They are simultaneously interpreting what they read. The other day we read a portion of Jesus' Sermon on the Mount from Matthew 5. Jesus' hyperboles in 5:29 about gouging out one's right eye or in 5:30 regarding cutting off one's right hand needed explanation and interpretation. They were rightly terrified and confused as they tried to make sense of Jesus' words. Immediately afterward, we entered into a conversation about how the Bible affects the way we choose to live our lives and Jesus' description of how much God hates our sin, not that he literally wants us to hurt ourselves. A correct interpretation is critical for children just as it is for adults.

A discussion of the characteristics of faithful preaching begins with faithful exegesis and interpretation. Effective preachers have a hunger for God's truth and for interpreting Scripture accurately and faithfully. Biblical preaching is synonymous with a commitment to solid biblical exegesis and interpretation as the first step, rather than beginning with the gauntlets of contrarian views heaved on us by the wider contemporary culture. This chapter provides a basic template for how to interpret Scripture faithfully with reference to doing our due diligence in determining the biblical author's intent in writing the text.

> While we can't understand everything in Scripture with perfect precision, we *can* understand a great deal once we connect to the worldview and outlook of the [biblical] writers.
>
> Michael S. Heiser, *The Bible Unfiltered*

We all recognize that the approach, method, or philosophy of interpreting Scripture will vary depending on who is speaking or writing.[1] Some may argue that it is impossible for a twenty-first-century preacher to be able to understand the biblical author's purpose or motivation for writing.[2] To a certain extent, they are correct. It is unviable for preachers today to understand *completely* a biblical author's context and meaning.

---

[1] Raymond Bailey, *Hermeneutics for Preaching: Approaches to Contemporary Interpretations of Scripture* (Nashville: Broadman, 1992); contributors provide seven different models of hermeneutics: (1) a historical model, (2) a canonical model, (3) a literary model, (4) a rhetorical model, (5) an African American model, (6) a philosophical model, and (7) a theological model.
[2] A chief concern for some interpreters is to determine "what the author is *doing* with what he is saying in the specific pericope chosen for the sermon" (emphasis original). See Abraham Kuruvilla, *Privilege the Text: A Theological Hermeneutic for Preaching* (Chicago: Moody, 2013), 25.

Does that mean we throw up our arms and give up? No, we still exercise the skills of biblical exegesis and ask the Holy Spirit to help us interpret accurately. Then we preach our best interpretation of the passage. As Michael S. Heiser writes: "While we can't understand everything in Scripture with perfect precision, we *can* understand a great deal once we connect to the worldview and outlook of the [biblical] writers."[3]

SELECTING A PASSAGE

Before we interpret a text for preaching, we need to select one.[4] How does one go about selecting a text for a sermon? It depends on our philosophy or method of text selection. Some choose to preach verse by verse through a book. The benefit of verse-by-verse exposition is that the preacher and listeners can't cherry-pick which verses to preach or listen to. The challenge of going through an entire book is that it may take years to finish a single book.

Others use the lectionary as a guide. What's helpful about the lectionary is that it offers a systematic way to preach through many portions of Scripture following a three-year cycle. It attempts to provide a broad diet of Scripture passages by including verses from four types of genres: an Old Testament reading (something from the Pentateuch or historical narratives, for example),

---

[3]Michael S. Heiser, *The Bible Unfiltered: Approaching Scripture on Its Own Terms* (Bellingham, WA: Lexham, 2017).

[4]For additional assistance on selecting a preaching text, see Haddon W. Robinson, *Biblical Preaching: The Development and Delivery of Expository Messages,* 3rd ed. (Grand Rapids: Baker, 2014), 29-33; chapter three of Bryan Chapell, *Christ-Centered Preaching: Redeeming the Expository Sermon,* 3rd ed. (Grand Rapids: Baker Academic, 2018); and H. B. Charles Jr., *On Preaching: Personal and Pastoral Insights for the Preparation and Practice of Preaching* (Chicago: Moody, 2014), 54-57.

a Proverb or Psalm, a Gospel reading, and a selection from one of the Epistles. Since it's not exhaustive, however, the drawback is that there will be verses and books that will not get preached for years and in some cases ever.

Sometimes preachers will choose to preach a topical sermon series on apologetics, human life, giving, stewardship, missions, evangelism, creation care, singleness, parenting, sexuality, or other subjects and choose an appropriate "best" text or texts for that particular sermon. Topical sermons and sermon series are helpful for biblical living and have become a staple in many churches, especially nondenominational churches. Some local situations as well as national or global crises will require the preacher to preach on an immediate concern, such as a natural disaster, tragedy, or other hardship, using a topical sermon. Although beneficial when done effectively, the dangers of topical preaching are noteworthy: choosing the wrong text, mishandling the text, misapplying the text, and proof texting (misusing a verse or passage out of context in order to fit our sermonic need). It's also quite easy to quickly gloss over several passages that have related themes without going into depth and explaining exegetical details.

There is no foolproof way to select a passage. Every preacher will develop a preferred method. However, we can guard against proof texting. Perhaps one of the most important considerations is determining whether or not a passage is a "unit of thought" that communicates a major, central, or big idea.[5] This could be a single verse, a few verses, a paragraph, a Psalm, a parable, a

---

[5]See Robinson, *Biblical Preaching*, 17-20, 29-30.

chapter or even chapters, especially when preaching from historical narratives. One might even be able to preach a sermon on the unit of thought of an entire book such as one of the Minor Prophets or a short Epistle.

A sermon's length will also determine how many verses one should try to expound in a given message. Does your tradition preach sermons that are more like homilies of eight to twelve minutes? Is a typical sermon twenty minutes, thirty to thirty-five minutes, forty to forty-five minutes, or longer? How much expositional depth can one address based on the number of verses and the length of the sermon? Many preachers bite off too much text that they and their listeners cannot possibly chew or digest. The length of the sermon will serve as your governing metric with regard to how much text is sufficient and appropriate.

THE SCHOOLS OF INTERPRETATION: ANTIOCH VERSUS ALEXANDRIA

Two schools of interpretation emerged in the second century, and they continue to characterize two broad approaches to interpreting Scripture: the School of Antioch in Syria, which championed a literal interpretation of Scripture, and the School of Alexandria in Egypt, which espoused an allegorical hermeneutic.[6] The sharp intellectual contrasts between the two schools are significant when it comes to personal interpretation or interpreting for preaching. The origin of the word *hermeneutics* or *interpretation* comes from

---

[6]See Walter C. Kaiser Jr., and Moisés Silva, *An Introduction to Biblical Hermeneutics: The Search for Meaning* (Grand Rapids: Zondervan, 1994), 211-28.

Hermes, "the messenger of the Greek gods."[7] Raymond Bailey explains, "Hermes invented language as the means of accomplishing his mission. He would not disclose the message to anyone except the one for whom it was intended; therefore, language had ambiguity enough for misunderstanding. The preacher is a messenger divinely charged with delivering the correct message to those for whom it was intended."[8] In order to deliver the message today, one must be a faithful interpreter of Scripture whether one ascribes to the Antiochian or Alexandrian philosophy.[9]

WHAT SHADE IS YOUR CULTURAL LENS?

The starting point for any faithful biblical interpretation is the nature and authority of the biblical text.[10] If one does not believe that God's Word is completely trustworthy and true, he or she will deem Scripture unreliable—thus rendering it unpreachable. The "alive and active" Word of God (Heb 4:12) is the foundation of faithful preaching, for God has revealed himself to us in Scripture. Without affirming its authority over us, even—or especially—the preacher, then our preaching is destined to fail. Incredulity toward the Bible will steer one toward other false interpretations. Do you remember what happened to Adam and Eve in the Garden of Eden in Genesis 3? The serpent asks a disruptive question using four words to split the minds of Eve and

---

[7] Bailey, *Hermeneutics for Preaching*, 8.
[8] Bailey, *Hermeneutics for Preaching*, 8-9.
[9] The author holds to the Antiochian philosophy of interpreting Scripture.
[10] The author believes that the Bible is both inerrant (without error) and infallible (useful and trustworthy) in the original languages.

Adam, "Did God really say . . . ?"[11] These four words have changed the trajectory of human existence. They continue to divide Christians even today about what God says in his Word.

> For the word of God is alive and active. Sharper than any double-edged sword, it penetrates even to dividing soul and spirit, joints and marrow; it judges the thoughts and attitudes of the heart.
>
> *Hebrews 4:12*

Since the 1970s, advocacy groups such as feminist and liberation approaches to hermeneutics have become popular trends seeking to advance their particular cause.[12] Later in the 1990s, other groups emerged, like postcolonial interpretations as well as LGBT interpretations, that have enabled marginalized communities.[13] In considering one's socio-ethno-cultural background, other hermeneutics such as African American, Hispanic American, and Asian American interpretive methods have come to the fore that consider how race, ethnicity, or culture influences

---

[11]Matthew Barrett makes a similar observation in *God's Word Alone: The Authority of Scripture* (Grand Rapids: Zondervan, 2016), 168.

[12]See, for example, the leading voices in these movements, such as Elisabeth Schüssler Fiorenza, *Wisdom Ways: Introducing Feminist Biblical Interpretation* (Maryknoll, NY: Orbis, 2001); Rosemary Radford Ruether, *Sexism and God Talk: Toward a Feminist Theology* (Boston: Beacon, 1993); Leonardo Boff and Clodovis Boff, *Introducing Liberation Theology* (Maryknoll, NY: Orbis, 1987); and Gustavo Gutiérrez, *A Theology of Liberation: History, Politics, and Salvation* (Maryknoll, NY: Orbis, 1988).

[13]William W. Klein, Craig L. Blomberg, and Robert L. Hubbard Jr., *Introduction to Biblical Interpretation*, 3rd ed. (Grand Rapids: Zondervan, 2017), 144-45.

one's interpretation.[14] There are important lessons that we can learn from these perspectives about how God's Word speaks to each of us in our particular contexts. At the same time, whenever race, ethnicity, or culture becomes the primary agenda and the primary lens through which to read the text rather than advancing God's kingdom and declaring the good news of Jesus Christ, we become less faithful interpreters of the text.

The reality is that every person reads Scripture through a particular lens. This lens often stems from one's core or dominant identity. Awareness of and attention to our own perspective—our own cultural lens—can help us as we seek to interpret the text. The problem becomes when the lens blurs or obstructs our vision of what God's Word says objectively. Part of the challenge, as Herman Bavinck writes, is that "the battle against the Bible is, in the first place, a revelation of the hostility of the human heart."[15] What, then, might be a more effective and faithful approach to Scripture interpretation?

---

[14]See Will Coleman, *Tribal Talk: Black Theology, Hermeneutics, and African/American Ways* (University Park, PA: The Pennsylvania State University, 2000); Frank A. Thomas, *Introduction to the Practice of African American Preaching* (Nashville: Abingdon, 2016); Francisco Lozada Jr., and Fernando F. Segovia, eds., *Latino/a Biblical Hermeneutics: Problematics, Objectives, Strategies* (Atlanta: SBL Press, 2014); Justo L. González and Pablo A. Jiménez, *Púlpito: An Introduction to Hispanic Preaching* (Nashville: Abingdon, 2005); Mary F. Foskett and Jeffrey Kah-Jin Kuan, eds., *Asian American Biblical Interpretation* (St. Louis: Chalice, 2006); and Matthew D. Kim and Daniel L. Wong, *Finding Our Voice: A Vision for Asian North American Preaching* (Bellingham, WA: Lexham, 2020).

[15]Herman Bavinck, *Reformed Dogmatics*, vol. 1, *Prolegomena*, ed. John Bolt, trans. John Vriend (Grand Rapids: Baker Academic, 2003), 440.

Common Interpretive Processes

Biblical scholars commonly recommend some variation of a ten-step or twelve-step process of interpreting Scripture.[16] As recent examples, Jason S. DeRouchie and Andrew David Naselli encourage similar but slightly different interpretive processes exploring the following: (1) genre, (2) textual criticism, (3) translation, (4) grammar, (5) argument diagram, (6) historical or historical-cultural context, (7) literary context, (8) word studies, (9) biblical theology, (10) historical theology, (11) systematic theology, and (12) practical theology.[17] In a pastor's week, it is nearly impossible to grapple for hours on end regarding each of these twelve topics—unless that is all that the pastor does! However, the astute preacher will want to spend *some* portion of the week thinking about each aspect of this process, giving greater precedence and time to certain topics more than others in a given sermon. The goal of biblical interpretation for the preacher is not to write a fifteen- to twenty-page exegetical paper but rather to write a sermon and prepare to preach a sermon.

---

[16]See, for example, Douglas Stuart, *Old Testament Exegesis: A Handbook for Students and Pastors*, 4th ed. (Louisville: Westminster John Knox, 2009) and Gordon Fee, *New Testament Exegesis: A Handbook for Students and Pastors*, 3rd ed. (Louisville: Westminster John Knox, 2002). Craig Keener and Jennifer Foutz Markley recommend a ten-step process of hermeneutics: (1) textual criticism, (2) translation and translations, (3) historical-cultural context, (4) literary context, (5) word studies, (6) grammar, (7) interpretive problems, (8) outlining, (9) theology, and (10) application. See Craig Keener and Jennifer Foutz Markley, *A Handbook for New Testament Exegesis* (Grand Rapids: Baker Academic, 2010).

[17]See Jason S. DeRouchie, *How to Understand and Apply the Old Testament: Twelve Steps from Exegesis to Theology* (Phillipsburg, NJ: P&R, 2017) and Andrew David Naselli, *How to Understand and Apply the New Testament: Twelve Steps from Exegesis to Theology* (Phillipsburg, NJ: P&R, 2017).

A WHOLE NEW "BIBLICAL" WORLD: INTERSECTIONS OF BIBLICAL STUDIES, THEOLOGY, AND PRACTICAL THEOLOGY

Certain shifts in biblical scholarship are evident over the last few decades. Pete Ward, in his book *Introducing Practical Theology*, observes that biblical studies is no longer a self-contained discipline and that interpretation invites conversations with other disciplines like theology, ecclesiology, and practical theology.[18] In particular, Ward names cross-fertilization, such as the sociology of the New Testament theological interpretation of Scripture, and collaborative hermeneutical models as church communities interpret Scripture together.[19] Furthermore, Larry W. Caldwell observes the hermeneutical trend toward ethnohermeneutics, which he defines as "Bible interpretation done in multigenerational, multicultural, and cross-cultural contexts and that, as far as possible, uses dynamic hermeneutical methods that already reside in the culture. Its primary goal is to interpret and communicate the truths of the Bible in ways that will be best understood by the receptor culture."[20]

The reason why preaching is exciting is because it blends all of these important disciplines in the life of the church. Preaching, in its best form, is the cross-pollination of biblical studies (Old

---

[18]Pete Ward, *Introducing Practical Theology: Mission, Ministry, and the Life of the Church* (Grand Rapids: Baker Academic, 2017), 121-24.

[19]Ward, *Introducing Practical Theology*, 122-23. See also Andrew P. Rogers, *Congregational Hermeneutics: How Do We Read?* (New York: Routledge, 2016).

[20]Larry W. Caldwell, "Missiology Toward Ethnohermeneutics: Contextualization 2.0 and Beyond," *Didaktikos: Journal of Theological Education* 3, no. 1 (March 2018): 37-38.

Testament and New Testament studies), theology (biblical, historical, and systematic), and practical theology (counseling, ecclesiology, ethics, educational ministry, and homiletics). Although there is no single, only, or "best" way to interpret Scripture, and although denominational and theological nuances will inevitably shape our reading, in the remaining parts of this chapter, I would like to suggest a hermeneutical process for those engaged in the work of intersecting hermeneutics with homiletics.

TOWARD AN AUTHORIAL-CULTURAL MODEL OF HERMENEUTICS

In *Preaching with Cultural Intelligence: Understanding the People Who Hear Our Sermons*, I recommend a five-step process of biblical interpretation for preaching using the acronym HABIT: **h**istorical, grammatical, and literary study; **a**uthor's cultural context; **b**ig idea of the text; **i**nterpret in your context; and **t**heological presuppositions.[21]

I will follow the same pattern here as I outline a basic template for moving from hermeneutics to homiletics. I often tell my students to avoid the temptation to move too quickly from hermeneutics to homiletics. Stay in the biblical world as long as you can to glean as much information as possible about your passage. How can we preach God's Word if we do not know what it says and means? A helpful rule of thumb is to spend as much time in exegesis as you do in preparing the outline and manuscript (for example, six hours in exegesis and six hours on homiletics).

---

[21]See Kim, *Preaching with Cultural Intelligence* (Grand Rapids: Baker Academic, 2017), 31-44.

HISTORICAL, GRAMMATICAL, AND LITERARY STUDY

As we said earlier, preaching begins with a proper understanding of the Scriptures. In order to understand the text, we should begin with studying the history, grammar, and literary context of the passage. Being faithful biblical expositors and preachers means starting here: with the text.

Start by reading the passage in a few different English translations. This will enable you to get the flow of the passage. You may want to read a more literal translation like the New American Standard Bible (NASB), a more dynamic equivalent translation like the New International Version (NIV), and perhaps even a paraphrase or application-oriented translation such as Eugene Peterson's *The Message*. In your notes, jot down any translation differences, difficulties, and questions along the way.

Second, learn about the historical context of your biblical author. Whenever someone writes a book or a letter, he or she has a purpose in mind for writing. We usually do not write someone without a reason. Gone are the days of handwritten letters (for the most part), but historically letter writing was the primary mode of communication. The purpose behind the letter may have been to communicate how much one missed or loved the other, or perhaps to update them on life, or to share one's plans with them. Bible commentaries typically have sections on the historical context, adding color and background information on the author's setting and the purpose behind the book or letter.

Third, study the grammar of the passage. Depending on your dexterity with the biblical languages and perhaps with assistance from Bible software such as Accordance or Logos, translate your text from the original Hebrew or Greek. Here you will want to consider the grammatical issues and sentence structure. For those who haven't learned the original languages, you should consider the benefits that such knowledge can bring. In the meantime, word studies are always beneficial to see how often a word is used, what its meaning or range of meaning is, where else it has been used, and more.

Fourth, literary genres also matter, so we want to become familiar with the various ways biblical genres can aid one's interpretation.[22] The literary genre of the passage may be narrative, poetry, gospel, epistle, apocalyptic, wisdom, or more. Each of these genres has its unique interpretive concerns and challenges.

AUTHOR'S CULTURAL CONTEXT

Second, we want to learn more about the author's cultural context. As we preach on a specific text, familiarizing ourselves with the author's culture is often something preachers gloss over. For instance, imagine that you are preaching a sermon on the book of Jonah.[23] While we know that Jonah was angry with God because of his mercy toward the Ninevites, what was he really so upset about? We often attribute Jonah's rancor toward God to his own ethnocentrism and even hedonism. However, there must be

---

[22]For help with literary genres, see Jeffrey D. Arthurs, *Preaching with Variety: How to Re-create the Dynamics of Biblical Genres* (Grand Rapids: Kregel, 2007).

[23]As an example, read my sermon and interview on "Jonah's Shady Outlook from His Sunny Lookout: Jonah 1-4," *Models for Biblical Preaching: Expository Sermons from the Old Testament*, eds. Haddon W. Robinson and Patricia Batten (Grand Rapids: Baker Academic, 2014), 159-72.

more to the story. Was Jonah scared of the Ninevites, was he angry at the Assyrians' horrific treatment of the Jews, or something else?

As we explore Nineveh in greater depth, we see that Nineveh was a major city in Assyria. What we discover in further researching of the Assyrians is that they tortured the Jews.[24] The physical and emotional torture of the Jews at the hands of the Assyrians was despicable. Imagine people from your culture being treated this way! No wonder Jonah feared them so much.

Most preachers will not think or bother to explore the cultural context of Nineveh or Assyria in detail beyond perhaps a geographic awareness. However, biblical authors recorded these details for a purpose. Scripture is steeped in cultural context. Yes, it takes some effort on our part, but we want to consider more deeply the cultural context of the author and the setting of the biblical account. Once we do so, we will have something to say to our listeners regarding the similarities and differences we share with the biblical world.[25] Whom might we similarly fear today?

BIG IDEA OF THE TEXT

Third, determine the big idea or main idea of the text. My preaching professor, Haddon W. Robinson, once explained how one locates the main idea in a given pericope by asking two questions of the text: (1) What is the author talking about? What

---

[24]See Erika Bleibtreu, "Grisly Assyrian Record of Torture and Death," in *Biblical Archaeology Review* (January/February 1991), 52-61.

[25]A helpful resource for understanding the author's cultural context is the *NIV Cultural Backgrounds Study Bible* (Grand Rapids: Zondervan, 2016).

Robinson referred to as the *subject question*, and (2) What is the author saying about what he's talking about? This was named by Robinson as the *complement answer*. By asking the subject question and answering with its complement answer, the preacher can discern the big idea, main idea, or exegetical idea.[26]

What could we say is the big idea of the entire book of Jonah? The subject question might be: Why does God send Jonah to the Ninevites? The complement is: because God shows compassion and mercy toward anyone that he wills, even Jonah's enemies, and he desires Jonah's obedience to share the good news with them so they repent. The full exegetical idea would be: God sends Jonah to the Ninevites because he shows compassion and mercy toward anyone he wills, even Jonah's enemies, and he desires Jonah's obedience to share the good news with them so that they repent.

INTERPRET IN YOUR CONTEXT

Fourth, it is not enough to know only what God said in his Word to the ancient Jews and first-century Christians. We want to take the next step and interpret Scripture in our own context. Donald Sunukjian summarizes the interpretive process in two phrases. First, he says, "Look at what God is saying . . ." and second, "Look at what God is saying . . . to us!"[27] The temptation for many preachers, in particular, and for Christians, in general, is to read the Bible focusing on the second phrase only and skipping the first. This shortcut is what has led many to fall into faulty exegesis.

---

[26]For additional assistance, see Robinson, *Biblical Preaching*, 15-26.

[27]Sunukjian, *Invitation to Biblical Preaching: Proclaiming Truth with Clarity and Relevance* (Grand Rapids: Kregel, 2007), 7.

Once we understand as best as we can what God's Word said to its original hearers and readers, we can shift our attention to today's listeners. Here are three questions we might ask of the text from the perspective of our hearers: (1) What are their assumptions? (2) What are their concerns? (3) What are their questions? Again, every single person reads the text through a particular lens. Anticipating their assumptions, concerns, and questions will enable us to better interpret the passage for the people in our contexts.[28] This will require background knowledge of our listeners. Turning again to Jonah, some interpretive questions might include: Are we running from God or reluctant to follow God's will in some area of our Christian life? Who do we fear? What types of people is it difficult to share the gospel with? Am I concerned more about the salvation of others or my own comfort? Whom do I need to love?

THEOLOGICAL PRESUPPOSITIONS

Finally, it is helpful to remember that preaching is about God. He is the central character in every part of Scripture. How does this particular biblical text speak of God? What presuppositions do we have about who God is in this pericope? Our theological presuppositions often shape how we preach the sermon. We want to consider both the positive and negative views of God in the text and acknowledge some of these views in the message itself. Our listeners will have their own sets of theological presuppositions. What are they? Somewhere in the sermon we can openly communicate our thoughts and their thoughts about God.

---

[28]See Kim, *Preaching with Cultural Intelligence*, 17-18.

Maybe, like Jonah, we've been thinking of God as a tyrant who forces us to do difficult or seemingly impossible things; perhaps we view God as overly merciful to the point of overlooking heinous sins. We may even think that God is abusive, fickle, wishy-washy, too stern or too lax, or other qualities, depending on our cultural context.

Conclusion

Faithful interpretation is the first key to effective preaching. We want to get the meaning of the text right. Just as the slightest coordinate will steer a ship or a plane off course, misunderstanding or mishandling Scripture misguides our listeners to the wrong isle or even the wrong continent, spiritually speaking. Not only is faithful interpretation absolutely critical, we also want to exegete our listeners' cultural context.

5

FAITHFUL
CULTURAL EXEGESIS

■■■

IN THE BACKYARD, our three boys have discovered numerous anthills. It seems to me that churches may resemble ant colonies. Unless you are a myrmecologist (i.e., an ant expert), all members of an ant colony look nearly indistinguishable. Some are slightly longer or shorter, while others are more narrow or round. From our limited perspective, every ant looks identical. But they're not! Each ant is unique and different. They have individual bodies, individual shapes and sizes, individual antennae, and individual patterns of movement. Sometimes we treat our congregations like ant colonies, thinking that every person is the same. They're not! Every congregation consists of people from different personal experiences, cultures, and backgrounds, even if outwardly they seem homogeneous.

In the previous chapter, we considered the first key element for faithful preaching—faithful interpretation. Preaching also requires specialized knowledge of one's congregational culture. Skye Jethani says, "No matter how hard it tries, the church will never be as cool as the culture. Relevance is a race it cannot win. In our attempts to compete with the culture we risk losing sight of the only thing of value the church has to offer the world—Jesus Christ."[1] He is right. The battle in the pulpit relates not to putting on True Religion jeans, sporting trendy tattoos, or having twenty thousand or more followers on Twitter, Instagram, or Snapchat.

Perhaps more than ever, preachers need to be faithful in cultural exegesis. Some might describe cultural exegesis as having cultural intelligence or cultural sensitivity.[2] Others might call cultural exegesis a more technical term like *ecclesiological ethnography*.[3] Our goal is not to compete with the culture but rather to comprehend the culture for the sake of effective proclamation of God's Word.[4] The point of this chapter is to remind us of seven broad groups of listeners who we might exegete and analyze in order to preach well-informed and well-aimed sermons.

WHO ARE THE PEOPLE IN YOUR NEIGHBORHOOD?

I grew up watching the television show *Mister Rogers' Neighborhood*. On that show, Fred Rogers usually took a stroll around his neighborhood to see who his neighbors were and befriend them. The beauty of the Mister Rogers show was all of the

---

[1]Skye Jethani, (@SkyeJethani) Twitter, January 19, 2018, 9:24 a.m.

[2]For specific help on how to engage in cultural exegesis, see Kim, *Preaching with Cultural Intelligence* (Grand Rapids: Baker Academic, 2017).

[3]Nicholas Healy, *Church, World and the Christian Life: Practical-Prophetic Ecclesiology* (Cambridge: Cambridge University Press, 2000), 168-69, in Pete Ward, *Introducing Practical Theology: Mission, Ministry, and the Life of the Church* (Grand Rapids: Baker Academic, 2017), 124.

[4]You may want to refresh your memory on Richard Niebuhr's five-fold typology on culture: Christ against culture, Christ of culture, Christ above culture, Christ and culture paradox, and Christ transforms culture. See Richard Niebuhr, *Christ and Culture* (New York: HarperCollins, 1951).

interesting personalities and characters who were part of his neighborhood—a microcosm of real communities. Fred Rogers made the effort to engage with and learn about those in his world, and we should do the same as preachers.

A Biblically Illiterate Culture

We are living in a biblically illiterate world. Gone are the days where we can assume any biblical knowledge from visitors or even weathered Christians. Many people today cannot name half of the Ten Commandments, half of the twelve disciples, and some may even believe that the Trinity is the name of a trendy rock band. Knowing our listeners' level of biblical literacy is one of the first features we might consider in terms of cultural exegesis. Depending on whether they are churched or unchurched, preachers may want to gauge the congregation's biblical awareness.

Not that we must be compelled to sponsor Bible trivia nights or Scripture memory competitions, but it's helpful in preaching to be cognizant of what our congregants recognize and are familiar with concerning God's Word. One way to discern how much of the Scriptures our listeners comprehend would be to give the church a short anonymous Bible quiz with ten to twenty multiple-choice questions. Yes, that's the seminary professor in me speaking. In any event, we might be pitching our sermons at an inappropriate scriptural level by aiming too high or too low with regard to our congregation's biblical and spiritual maturity.[5]

---

[5]See Scott M. Gibson, *Preaching with a Plan: Sermon Strategies for Growing Mature Believers* (Grand Rapids: Baker Books, 2012), 27-28.

Even basic courtesies can help our listeners, such as giving pew Bible page numbers for sermon texts or explaining who certain characters are in the Bible and summarizing the narratives that we, who have grown up in the church, take for granted.

GENERATIONAL CULTURES

Congregational demographics can be age specific by having a narrow age range.[6] For instance, some churches, especially in university or college towns, cater toward millennials, who are often college, university, or graduate students. Others are primarily Generation X married couples with or without children in their thirties, forties, or fifties. Some congregations include mainly baby boomers who are now in their fifties, sixties, or seventies. Lastly, churches in North America can be what some call "silver" churches—those who are septuagenarians, octogenarians, and nonagenarians. Most likely, your local congregation is to some degree intergenerational, which means you must become fluent across the generations. How we speak to millennials will be noticeably different from boomers and even more so from builders. This will take some concerted effort to be able to preach to both sides of the aisles.

In the epistles, Paul reminds Titus of the importance and even necessity of intergenerational ministry for the life of the church.

---

[6]Common designations for generations are builders, the institutional generation (1901-1924); the silent generation, bridge builders (1925-1942); baby boomers, visionaries and seekers (1943-1961/64); Generation X, a relational generation (1961/64-1981); the millennial generation, young navigators (1981-1999); and Generation Z (2000-present). See Andrew Carl Wisdom, *Preaching to a Multi-generational Assembly* (Collegeville, MN: Liturgical, 2004), 81.

He instructs older men to model the faith to younger men by living as leaders who are "temperate, worthy of respect, self-controlled, and sound in faith, in love and in endurance" (Titus 2:2). He calls for older women in the faith to lead by example as well as "to be reverent in the way they live, not to be slanderers or addicted to much wine, but to teach what is good" (Titus 2:3). Then, Paul charges Titus, "In everything set them an example by doing what is good. In your teaching show integrity, seriousness and soundness of speech that cannot be condemned, so that those who oppose you may be ashamed because they have nothing bad to say about us" (Titus 2:7-8).

In these important verses, Paul provides a clear model for intergenerational ministry. He also resets our focus to say, remember preachers and pastors, you set the tone for the rest of the congregation by teaching sound doctrine and living as God's sanctified leaders. J. Brian Tucker and John Koessler rightly observe, "It is certainly not a calculation that can be made with scientific precision, because generational differences are more a matter of perception than biology. . . . While there are always exceptions among individuals, each collective generation does seem to have certain characteristics that set it apart from the others."[7] Therefore, we want to exegete and understand these generational differences.[8]

---

[7]J. Brian Tucker and John Koessler, *All Together Different: Upholding the Church's Unity While Honoring Our Individual Identities* (Chicago: Moody, 2018), 186.

[8]A helpful resource for generational exegesis is Elisabeth A. Nesbit Sbanatto and Craig L. Blomberg, *Effective Generational Ministry: Biblical and Practical Insights for Transforming Church Communities* (Grand Rapids: Baker Academic, 2016).

SECULAR CULTURES

Increasingly, we are preaching to listeners who hold to various secular worldviews. Some of these designations include people who are not religious, also known as *nones, postmodernists, skeptics, apathetics, agnostics, atheists,* and even *the hostile.* The challenge is to anticipate their presuppositions, questions, concerns, and challenges regarding Scripture and God's message to them. J. Ellsworth Kalas writes, "Secularism and materialism, the formidable graven images of our day, increase daily in numbers and in their appeal. The overall moral culture of our society seems more corrupting year after year."[9] We sense this moral decay and irreverence for God and God's Word daily. Secular listeners and sometimes even churched ones do not accept prima facie interpretations of Scripture. Secular culture has taught them that their lived experience trumps our loyal exegesis. Our proclamation cannot afford to ignore secular cultures.[10]

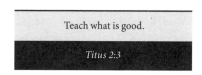

Teach what is good.

Titus 2:3

ETHNIC AND RACIAL CULTURES

The fourth category of culture can be a bit tricky, but it's crucial in our cultural exegesis. Ethnic and racial cultures are vastly different depending on one's ethnic and racial identity and affiliation.

---

[9] J. Ellsworth Kalas, *Preaching in an Age of Distraction* (Downers Grove, IL: InterVarsity Press, 2014), 130.

[10] See Phil Zuckerman, *Living the Secular Life: New Answers to Old Questions* (New York: Penguin, 2014).

While many congregations in North America are composed of a dominant ethnic or racial group, increasingly we see trends toward ethnic or racial diversity in our neighborhoods, including urban, suburban, and rural contexts. How do we relate to those from other ethnic and racial cultures? Do we consider them in our interpretation as well as proclamation? Are they embraced or ignored? Do we care to get to know them beyond stereotypical perceptions? Our job is not simply to get different people to sit in the same pews. Becoming familiar with ethnic and racial cultures can take extraordinary amounts of time and energy. Choose to learn proactively about those ethnic and racially different listeners with whom we do not share certain affinities but with whom we are also disciples of Jesus Christ.[11]

SOCIOECONOMIC AND EDUCATIONAL CULTURES

Another facet of cultural exegesis involves considering socioeconomic and educational differences. A preacher might think about using illustrations that her audience can identify and resonate with. Leonora Tubbs Tisdale shares about preaching in a rural context that was foreign to her experience: "On some Sundays, I felt that my sermons were 'missing' them altogether."[12] Application of financial stewardship looks differently depending

---

[11]For understanding the intersection between preaching and ethnicity, see chapter six in Kim, *Preaching with Cultural Intelligence*; and Matthew D. Kim, "The World of Ethnic and Cultural Issues in Preaching," in *The Worlds of the Preacher: Navigating Biblical, Cultural, and Personal Contexts*, ed. Scott M. Gibson (Grand Rapids: Baker Academic, 2018), 73-88.

[12]Leonora Tubbs Tisdale, *Preaching as Local Theology and Folk Art* (Minneapolis: Fortress, 1997), 3.

on who is listening: Is this person a single father or mother living on welfare, or are they financially secure? Cultural exegesis tells us that the socioeconomic level of our church influences the examples we employ from the pulpit. We might say *apartment* rather than *house*. We might say *bus* rather than *car* and vice versa. Urban city dwellers and rural people may not appreciate excessive pontification about narrow topics of interest that are not applicable to them. In the same way, we want to exegete the educational backgrounds of our listeners. A recent *Forbes* article reports that most Americans do not have a bachelor's degree.[13] The assumption that many pastors make is that our church members are college educated. Preachers commonly say things such as, "When you were in college . . ." Although we might assume some level of college education in particular contexts, cultural exegesis confirms that not everyone goes to college, earns a college degree, or goes on to business school, law school, medical school, or other types of graduate school. Keith Willhite reminds preachers, "From a communication perspective . . . *listeners* determine whether the sermon is relevant."[14] As such, faulty assumptions can leave the impression that more educated preachers (who have earned bachelor's, seminary master's degrees, and beyond) can appear snobbish, demeaning, arrogant, naive, irrelevant, and out-of-touch with the struggles and

---

[13]Andrew Kelly, "The Neglected Majority: What Americans Without a College Degree Think About Higher Education, Part 1," April 28, 2015, www.forbes.com/sites/akelly/2015/04/28/the-neglected-majority-what -americans-without-a-college-degree-think-about-higher-education -part-1/#1b71bf7172cf.

[14]Keith Willhite, *Preaching with Relevance: Without Dumbing Down* (Grand Rapids: Kregel, 2001), 21-22, emphasis original.

concerns of "real people." By all means, if your congregation is more educated, meet them where they are. But if they are not, then you should be sensitive to speak to them with dignity and in educationally and culturally germane ways.

> *Listeners* determine whether the sermon is relevant.
>
> Keith Willhite, *Preaching with Relevance*

THE LEAST OF THESE CULTURES

A final, often-omitted cultural feature regards what Jesus calls "the least of these" in Matthew 25:40. Today, the term "least of these" can come across the wrong way. Please do not misunderstand me. I am referring to those who are frequently ignored, marginalized, or ostracized in society and in the church: the mentally and physically disabled and handicapped, those with Down syndrome, autoimmune-disease sufferers, those with chronic illness, the blind, the deaf, the bedridden, the paralyzed, the physically deformed, the limbless, the loveless, the autistic and those on the autism spectrum, the poor and impoverished, survivors of physical and sexual abuse, the displaced, immigrants, refugees, captives, and prisoners, veterans, the depressed and suicidal, LGBTQ, those who have lost a loved one, and others.

You might ask, "How can you lump all of these different types of people into one category? Doesn't that almost include everyone?" My rejoinder is, "How do we as a Christian community respond when someone from one of these 'least of these' cultures enters our church building and sanctuary?" In some manner, the least of these are individuals who are in need and for whatever reason are made to feel less than. Not turning anyone away, Jesus commonly asked, "What do you want me to do for you?" (Mk 10:36). Those who have experience with one or more of the above have greater empathy and patience than those who have not.

Several years ago, at the age of thirty-six, I suffered a blow to the head playing pick-up basketball. The ball struck me on the side of the head at full speed, leaving in its wake the lingering and debilitating effects of a concussion. Now seven years later, I still wake up every morning and go to bed every night dizzy. Every conscious moment I am suffering from chronic dizziness. A few months after this basketball injury, the doctors diagnosed me with glaucoma. This explained why I did not see the ball coming at my head due to significant loss of peripheral vision. I am bracing myself for the day when I may physically see no more.

On November 7, 2015, my younger brother Tim, who was living and working in Manila, Philippines, was out celebrating his thirty-sixth birthday. Later that night, some Filipinos brutally murdered him, eventually discarding his body from the twenty-third floor of his high-rise apartment complex approximately five hundred feet in the air—a fatal and crushing blow to the skull.

This horrific event and painful loss has deeply shaped who I am today. May I consider myself one of the least of these too? From these experiences, I have much more empathy and appreciation today for those who fit a "least of these" category than I ever did before. Exegeting the "least of these" will require investment of time and listening to their stories and pains, but they are worth every minute!

Conclusion

Faithful cultural exegesis is by no means limited to only these cultural groups. Other significant cultural contexts have not been broached, such as differing religious contexts, political ties, denominational affiliations, gender issues, and more generally various languages, customs, symbols, celebrations, cultural expressions, and more. Next time you preach, take a moment to see the beautiful faces in your congregation and determine which cultures will require your immediate cultural exegesis. See the *imago Dei* in them and love them by taking the time to listen to them, to understand them, value them, disciple them, shepherd them, and preach more effectively to them.

6

FAITHFUL
APPLICATION

■ ■ ■

I LOATHE PUTTING TOGETHER IKEA furniture. On a
pastor and professor's salary, our family has not always been
able to afford premade furnishings. IKEA's bare-bones, stick-
figure instructions are confusing for the average do-it-yourselfer.
To put together the final product, one must be able to interpret
and apply IKEA's instructions: a hodgepodge of particleboard;
different types of screws, nuts, and bolts; wooden dowels; tiny
nails; and several mysterious bits that you end up discarding in
sheer frustration.

The IKEA builder must first take requisite time to interpret
the diagrams. Your intuition only leads you astray. You have to
navigate which pieces go where and determine the all-important
question of which direction those arrows are pointing if you're
going to have any chance at constructing something usable. By-
passing this interpretative stage ultimately puts you as the furniture builder (and more importantly those who use the product)
in peril.

Infinitely more important than building IKEA furniture,
preaching requires faithful application of Scripture. The first step

of preaching is faithful interpretation, which we explored in chapter four. Then, in chapter five, we discussed the second step of preaching: faithful cultural exegesis. Third, we want to explore faithful application. What comes to your mind when you think of the word *application*?

To apply something means to exercise one's knowledge or ability by putting it into practice. We may hear listeners murmuring that the Bible is too difficult to understand. Yes, to some extent they are right in offering their lament. However, the reality is that the Bible is more difficult to apply than it is to comprehend. The Danish philosopher Søren Kierkegaard put it bluntly, "The Bible is very easy to understand. But we Christians are a bunch of scheming swindlers. We pretend to be unable to understand it because we know very well that the minute we understand, we are obliged to act accordingly."[1] Patricia M. Batten shares this memory: "In a 4 x 6 wooden frame perched on Haddon Robinson's desk was a little ditty: 'Tommy Snooks and Bessie Brooks were leaving church one Sunday. Said Tommy Snooks to Bessie Brooks, "Tomorrow will be Monday." She explains that "what is preached on Sunday must make a difference on Monday.""[2]

In this chapter, we will consider some necessary elements to faithful application and how we, as preachers, can put biblical truth into practice for ourselves and for our listeners on Monday morning and throughout the week.

---

[1] Søren Kierkegaard, *Provocations: Spiritual Writings of Kierkegaard*, ed. Charles E. Moore (Farmington, PA: Plough, 2002), 201.

[2] Patricia M. Batten, "An Apology for Learning Educational Theory," in *Training Preachers: A Guide to Teaching Homiletics*, ed. Scott M. Gibson (Bellingham, WA: Lexham, 2018), 28.

Is Application Necessary?

Over the years, some movers and shakers in mainline homiletics have questioned whether biblical application in the sermon is even necessary. For instance, David Randolph, David Buttrick, Fred Craddock, Eugene Lowry, and other members of the New Homiletic movement from the 1960s and beyond suggested moving away from sermon application.[3] In their view, the preacher's role is simply to help listeners make their own conclusions about how this text connects to their lived experiences. The preacher need not spend his or her time unpacking and communicating application for all. Similarly, with a de-emphasis on application, certain preachers from evangelical circles might contest that the purpose of preaching is to help "people encounter God through his word,"[4] placing the thrust of preaching on encountering God and not on personal or corporate application. Even further, some preachers might contend that sermon application may lead to moralism and legalism when it ought to be Christ-centered and gospel-centered.

---

[3]See, for instance, David J. Randolph, *The Renewal of Preaching in the Twenty-First Century: The Next Homiletics*, 2nd ed. (Eugene, OR: Cascade, 2009); David Buttrick, *Homiletic: Moves and Structures* (Philadelphia: Fortress, 1987); Fred B. Craddock, *Preaching* (Nashville: Abingdon, 1985); Eugene L. Lowry, *The Homiletical Plot: The Sermon as Narrative Art Form*, 2nd ed. (Louisville: Westminster John Knox, 2000); Lucy Atkinson Rose, *Sharing the Word: Preaching in the Roundtable Church* (Louisville: Westminster John Knox, 1997); and Alyce M. McKenzie, *Making a Scene in the Pulpit: Vivid Preaching for Visual Learners* (Louisville: Westminster John Knox, 2018).

[4]Jason C. Meyer, *Preaching: A Biblical Theology* (Wheaton, IL: Crossway, 2013), 21.

Faithful application, to put it plainly, is downright hard to do. Haddon Robinson once warned, "More heresy is preached in application than in Bible exegesis."[5] We can actually apply God's Word unfaithfully and not connect the application for people living in the biblical world with today's disparate peoples and their experiences. Some of these differences we noted in the previous chapter on faithful cultural exegesis. Yet we *can* say with confidence that the Scriptures must be faithfully applied to the lives of our listeners. As James says, "Do not merely listen to the word, and so deceive yourselves. Do what it says" (Jas 1:22). How, then, can we faithfully provide biblical application for our hearers?

APPLY THE ORIGINAL AUTHOR'S PURPOSE

We want to start this conversation by applying the original author's purpose. Chris Nye observes, "In America, we tend to be very utilitarian readers of Scripture. We ask questions such as, 'How is this text useful to me? What can I do with this passage in my life?' Those are not bad questions; however, we have made them a bit too central in our preaching and teaching."[6] Rather, faithful application begins not with me and us but with asking: Why did the biblical author pen their portion of the Scripture,

---

[5] Haddon W. Robinson, "The Heresy of Application: It's When We're Applying Scripture That Error Most Likely Creeps In," in *The Art and Craft of Biblical Preaching*, ed. Haddon W. Robinson and Craig Brian Larson (Grand Rapids: Zondervan, 2005), 306.

[6] Chris Nye goes on to argue that sermons should help listeners enjoy Scripture rather than focus on application. See Chris Nye, "Why I Gave Up Sermon Application," accessed March 22, 2018, www.preaching today.com/skills/2018/january/why-i-gave-up-sermon-application.html.

and to whom were they writing? Beyond the obvious answer that God instructed them to do so, the biblical authors had clear intentions and specific readers in mind for their book or letter.

For example, Luke records his primary purpose or thesis for writing his Gospel in the opening verses. He writes, "With this in mind, since I myself have carefully investigated everything from the beginning, I too decided to write an orderly account for you, most excellent Theophilus, so that you may know the certainty of the things you have been taught" (Lk 1:3-4). Luke's purpose for writing is to affirm and confirm Theophilus's knowledge of Christian teachings and faith. The corollary application would be that Theophilus could have assurance and certainty about God's instructions and his faith. This same purpose applies to us today. Whenever possible, we want to convey to our listeners today this same original author's purpose for writing.

A growing concern in homiletics as it relates to biblical interpretation and application concerns preachers who impose their theological presuppositions onto the text. No preacher can be impartial completely in his or her interpretation and application. We acknowledge this difficulty. We read the text with a particular preunderstanding based on our identity, culture, convictions, experiences, theology, and other factors.[7] Yet without our detection, sometimes we become accustomed to preaching a specific theological understanding of the text (for example, some form of biblical theology) rather than the intended meaning of

---

[7]See J. Scott Duvall and J. Daniel Hays, *Grasping God's Word: A Hands-On Approach to Reading, Interpreting, and Applying the Bible*, 3rd ed. (Grand Rapids: Zondervan, 2012), 139-40.

the biblical and divine authors.[8] This type of preaching is dangerous for the preacher and for the listeners.

APPLY *YOUR* TEXT

Second, faithful application involves applying the actual text on which we are preaching. A pet peeve of mine—and perhaps for you as well—is when preachers spend time in a particular passage of Scripture for their sermon but then pivot when it comes to application, asking, "How can we apply this text from Exodus 3? Let's turn to Mark 1." Preachers commonly preach from the Old Testament but then seek a New Testament passage for the application. It also happens when preachers have no idea how to apply a pericope. I firmly attest that Scripture interprets Scripture, so a christological reading of the Old Testament is certainly possible. However, why not apply *your* text? Paul reminds young Timothy that "all Scripture is God-breathed and is useful for teaching, rebuking, correcting and training in righteousness, so that the servant of God may be thoroughly equipped for every good work" (2 Tim 3:16-17). If we believe this, then we should be able to apply any text to the lives of our congregants.

Scott M. Gibson notices a common problem among preachers when he writes, "Preachers . . . let's determine to talk about the text. Talking about the text is our commitment. Talking about the text is our responsibility."[9] Gibson notes the prevalence of

---

[8]See Scott M. Gibson and Matthew D. Kim, eds., *Homiletics and Hermeneutics: Four Views on Preaching Today* (Grand Rapids: Baker Academic, 2018).

[9]See Scott M. Gibson, "Preach the Text," Preaching.com, accessed March 22, 2018, www.preaching.com/articles/preach-the-text/.

preachers preaching around the text, which resembles a ballroom dance where the sermon never touches the text like waltzing partners who never hold hands and connect with each other. When we preach Scripture, we determine the primary application from the passage and not from a secondary or tertiary source, which exacerbates speaking around the text.

APPLY THE TEXT TO *YOURSELF*

A third principle of faithful application is to apply the text to ourselves as preachers. The natural predilection for preachers is to think about the sermon application(s) for our hearers first before we consider application for our own lives. Robinson defined biblical or expository preaching as "the communication of a biblical concept, derived from and transmitted through a historical, grammatical, and literary study of a passage in its context, which the Holy Spirit *first applies to the personality and experience of the preacher*, then through the preacher, applies to the hearers."[10]

In applying the text to myself first, I allow God to transform my heart, mind, and will according to his truth in Scripture. A preacher who forgets or fails to apply God's Word is no better than a Bible travel guide who has never visited specific biblical landmarks in Bethlehem, Corinth, Jerusalem, or Rome. How can we lead others when we do not know where we are going or how we can get there? If we are vulnerable, we can admit that our human nature would rather focus on others' problems rather than dealing with our own sins. As Jesus confronts us, "You hypocrite, first take the plank out of your own eye, and then you

---

[10]Haddon W. Robinson, *Biblical Preaching: The Development and Delivery of Expository Messages,* 3rd ed. (Grand Rapids: Baker, 2014), 5, (emphasis added).

will see clearly to remove the speck from your brother's eye" (Mt 7:5). First, apply the Word to yourself, which is an important, initial part of the preaching process.

APPLY TO A SPECIFIC PERSON AND CULTURE

Once we apply the Word to our lives, we want to offer application for our hearers. One of the primary purposes of seeking to understand our listeners and exegete their cultures is to apply God's Word faithfully to their lives. At times, it can be overwhelming to think about all of the different types of listeners sitting in the pews. Application can invoke a form of preaching paralysis. How can I possibly apply God's Word to all people at once?

One way that I have found helpful to streamline the process is to apply the text with one specific person or cultural group in view. This seems counterintuitive because it seems no different from applying God's Word to myself and hoping that everyone else thinks and responds like me. However, my pulpit experience confirms that when I choose one person or group in the congregation and apply God's Word to them, God still communicates to others in his own way. I remember countless times when I applied God's Word to a certain individual in the church. After the sermon, other people (sometimes not even the individual I had in mind) would come up to me and say, "I felt like you wrote that sermon just for me."

Each week I encourage you to rotate and think about various types of listeners in your congregation for your sermon application(s). Consider shifting your applicational gaze in each sermon to various listeners in the church. Include everyone from the single dad to the seemingly perfect parents, from the Fortune 500 president to the local grocery store clerk, from the elderly widow to the unwed pregnant teen, from the mentally ill to the alpha female, from the closet alcoholic to the new convert who is on fire for Jesus, and a host of others. Apply the Word for a single individual or group, and see how the Holy Spirit works mysteriously to apply the Word to everyone's life as well.

> Use your home, apartment, dorm room, front yard, community gymnasium, or garden for the purpose of making strangers into neighbors and neighbors into family.
>
> Rosaria Butterfield,
> *The Gospel Comes with a House Key*

APPLY WITH VARIETY

Finally, there is no single way to apply Scripture. Variety in application is the key. First, perhaps to our surprise, application does not always involve communicating a list of one to three action steps in the conclusion. Sometimes application is more about *being* rather than *doing*.[11] Think of Luke's record of Mary and Martha's interaction with Jesus in their home (Lk 10:38-42). Mary sat at Jesus' feet to learn. The application has more to do with being with Jesus (Mary's example) rather than doing something for him (Martha's example). While Martha's character is often used as a negative example, it's clear that Jesus notices Martha's anxiety and commends her service but says that Mary has

---

[11]See Kim, *Preaching with Cultural Intelligence* (Grand Rapids: Baker Academic, 2017), 27.

chosen what is better. We want to have a balance of *being* versus *doing* applications.

Second, application is not always personal, but it is often communal. The individualistic culture in which we live lends itself toward a hyperindividualistic reading of Scripture. It is just "me and Jesus," as some say. When we look at various parts of Scripture, the application is in the form of you (plural) and not you (singular). For example, the early church in Acts 2 reveals the communal nature of what Christians should value and how they relate to each other. The "togetherness" of the early believers reminds us of an ancient antidote to modern individualism and even individual Christian piety. The original Christians saw one another's needs and met those needs as a community. They even enjoyed each other's company. They embodied the gospel in every sphere of life. Rosaria Butterfield encourages Christians in her book *The Gospel Comes with a House Key* to "use your home, apartment, dorm room, front yard, community gymnasium, or garden for the purpose of making strangers into neighbors and neighbors into family. Because that is the point—building the church and living like a family, the family of God."[12] In our sermons, we can remind today's Christians that application is similarly lived out in community.

Third, application leads to life transformation but is not a substitute for life transformation. This means the goal of preaching is not simply behavior modification. Changing behavior alone is not our ultimate end. Sometimes our preaching unintentionally

---

[12]Rosaria Butterfield, *The Gospel Comes with a House Key: Practicing Radically Ordinary Hospitality in Our Post-Christian World* (Wheaton, IL: Crossway, 2018), 14.

evokes a mental checklist of various behaviors needing altera-
tions. Rather, when we apply God's Word faithfully, we (including our listeners) will become more like Christ. Paul said to
the Corinthians, "Follow my example, as I follow the example of
Christ" (1 Cor 11:1). Every time we heed and apply God's Word,
we experience life transformation and grow in spiritual maturity.
The biblical application that we provide our listeners with each
week represents another piece of the puzzle moving them toward
spiritual wholeness, Christlikeness, and the abundant life that
Jesus promises, "I have come that they may have life, and have it
to the full" (Jn 10:10). The fullness of life comes from applying
God's Word rather than remaining stuck in the world and being
like the world.

> Students of preaching struggle with the application
> stage more than with any other area.
>
> Terry G. Carter, J. Scott Duvall, and J. Daniel Hays,
> *Preaching God's Word*

CONCLUSION

The culmination of effective preaching is faithful application.
The prerequisites for faithful application are faithful interpretation and faithful cultural exegesis. In this short chapter, we
have merely scratched the surface with respect to applying
Scripture in sermons. In *Preaching God's Word*, Carter, Duvall,
and Hays share from their experiences: "Through years of
teaching homiletics, we have discovered that students of

preaching struggle with the application stage more than with any other area."[13] I would add novice and experienced preachers to this student category as well. While no preacher is perfect in his or her application skills, the key is to remember to first apply Scripture to yourself and then do your best to apply God's truth to your hearers—the very souls God entrusts to your care.[14]

---

[13]Terry G. Carter, J. Scott Duvall, and J. Daniel Hays, *Preaching God's Word: A Hands-On Approach to Preparing, Developing, and Delivering the Sermon*, 2nd ed. (Grand Rapids: Zondervan, 2018), 117.

[14]See Robinson's definition of expository preaching, *Biblical Preaching*, 5.

PART THREE

CHARACTERISTICS OF FAITHFUL PREACHERS

7

BEING PASTORAL
AND LOVING

■ ■ ■

I ONCE HAD A STUDENT ask me in preaching class if it is possible that God permits a full-time vocation in itinerant preaching rather than having to serve as a local church pastor. When I asked him why, he responded with great candor, "I love to preach, but I don't like people." We cannot separate preaching from shepherding and loving God's people. Yet sometimes as preachers, we love to preach but fail to love the people to whom we preach. This chapter seeks to encourage preachers to have the heart of a pastor first where preaching is understood as just one expression of the pastor's calling.

WHY COMPARTMENTALIZE MINISTRY?

In the twenty-first century, the compartmentalization of pastoral ministry has become increasingly acute. Pastors serve in niche positions, such as assistant pastor, associate pastor, campus pastor, children's pastor, youth pastor, teaching pastor, educational ministries pastor, evangelism and discipleship pastor, pastor of small groups, counseling pastor, executive pastor, senior pastor, pastor for preaching and vision, solo pastor, college pastor, pastor of visitation, pastor of families, pastor of young adults, missions pastor, and so on.

The paradigm shift toward ministry compartmentalization has not always served the church well when it comes to cultivating our love and pastoral concern for *all* members of our congregation. We commonly limit our pastoral roles and responsibilities to our pastoral titles—even in our own minds. Our default mode becomes, "That's not part of *my* job description. Or *they* are not my responsibility." While I adopt the team ministry model, especially for larger congregations, our unique pastoral titles box us into specific roles or pigeonholes where we do not have freedom or time to think, dream, and minister holistically.

Pastors in previous eras of history viewed their pastoral work differently than we do today. We tend to view ministers as becoming specialists, filling a void or niche in church life. Historic pastors understood ministers as being generalists. For instance, the oft-mentioned Great Awakening pastor and theologian Jonathan Edwards served twenty-three years as the pastor of a Congregational church in Northampton, Massachusetts.[1] While Edwards receives much attention because of his rich theological works and his long catalog of published and unpublished sermons, he may not receive enough credit for his life as a pastoral shepherd.[2]

---

[1] Jonathan Edwards, preface to *Sermons of Jonathan Edwards* (Peabody, MA: Hendrickson, 2005), xiii.

[2] Edwards receives credit for 1,400 unpublished sermons. See Stephen J. Nichols, "Jonathan Edwards: His Life and Legacy," in *A God Entranced Vision of All Things: The Legacy of Jonathan Edwards*, eds. John Piper and Justin Taylor (Wheaton, IL: Crossway, 2004), 36.

Concerning Edwards's pastoral heart, Stephen J. Nichols reflects, "He was a pastor, and he had a deep and abiding concern for the spiritual state of those under his care."[3] Providing additional color to his pastoral life, Edward Panosian notes, "Physically frail most of his life, Edwards conserved his energy for what he believed was its most profitable use. Yet he always went to his people when sent for, to the sick and to the afflicted. And ministers and other dignitaries, when passing through, found—and often later wrote of—his cordial hospitality and gracious care and provision for their welfare."[4] Edwards, known to have frequently written his sermons standing up near a large window, would look out on the fields where some of his parishioners tilled the soil.[5] They saw him diligently working on his sermon through this porthole while he encouraged them as they worked persistently on producing crops for the Lord's people. While Edwards and other preachers of his generation are commonly referred to today as pastor theologians, they recognized and practiced the necessary and natural cross-fertilization between preaching and pastoral ministry. Pastors in prior eras viewed pastoral work holistically and not with an attitude of compartmentalization of ministry.

In his 1877 Yale *Lectures on Preaching*, Phillips Brooks forthrightly observed that "the work of the preacher and the pastor

---

[3] Nichols, "Jonathan Edwards: His Life and Legacy," 43.
[4] See Edward M. Panosian, "Jonathan Edwards: America's Theologian-Preacher," in *Faith of Our Fathers: Scenes from American Church History*, ed. Mark Sidwell (Greenville, SC: BJU Press, 1991), 33-39.
[5] See Matthew D. Kim, "Guard Your Sermon Preparation Time," in *Preaching Points: 55 Tips for Improving Your Pulpit Ministry*, ed. Scott M. Gibson (Wooster, OH: Weaver, 2016), 24.

really belong together, and ought not be separated. I believe that very strongly. . . . The preacher needs to be pastor, that he may preach to real men. The pastor must be preacher, that he may keep the dignity of his work alive. The preacher, who is not a pastor, grows remote. The pastor, who is not a preacher, grows petty. . . . Be both; for you cannot really be one unless you also are the other."[6] Why are the two inseparable? There are many reasons, but here are four that stand out.

> The preacher needs to be pastor. . . .
> The pastor must be preacher.
>
> Phillips Brooks, *Lectures on Preaching*

Pastoral warmth. Everybody needs love. The Beatles expressed this sentiment in their hit song, "All You Need Is Love." That ubiquitous craving for pure love includes every breathing person who walks into our church building. While expectations of pastors differ, people generally expect pastors to demonstrate love, warmth, and interest in their lives. The pastoral warmth that we show in the church narthex is the same preacher's warmth we should exhibit from the church pulpit. When there is disconnect, congregants feel the sting of insincerity.

Years ago, I sat under the preaching ministry of a godly pastor whose vocal chords reverberated primarily at one volume level— that of shouting. His countenance was on the more serious end of the spectrum, but people generally sensed his love. In conversations

---

[6]Phillips Brooks, *Lectures on Preaching* (New York: E. P. Dutton, 1877), 75-77.

in the fellowship hall, he would ask us questions about our lives and encourage us to grow closer to Jesus. Yet when he preached, listeners questioned his love. He would holler and turn rosy red in the cheeks in every sermon for extended periods during the sermon. For this pastor and preacher, "God loves you" sounded like a rancorous rebuke. The tone of our sermons matters. Even when communicating words of warning and correction, listeners ought to know and feel that they stem from our pastoral posture of love and grace. To expand on James's words, I would add, preaching warmth without pastoral warmth is dead.[7]

Pastoral directness. The Bible refers to people as sheep and to pastors as shepherds. The image, though off-putting at times, is quite apropos. In order to guide the sheep, the shepherd must know them and know them well. Haddon Robinson offered sage advice when he said, "The novice preacher asks first the question, 'What should I preach?' while the master preacher asks first, 'To whom am I preaching?'"[8] If we are not intentional in knowing the people, our sermons become steady doses of generic placebos that attempt to be one-cure-fits-all quick fixes rather than hitting the target of our listeners' spiritual maladies. Pastoral directness means the ability to be direct in our sermons because we are well acquainted with our listeners' conditions, concerns, and questions.

---

[7]I recognize that sometimes as pastors we struggle to love the flock. This happens to all pastors.

[8]Jeffrey Volkmer, "Theotechnos: Some Reflections on the Intersection of Social Media and Theology," *The Good Book Blog: Talbot School of Theology*, February 9, 2011, www.biola.edu/blogs/good-book-blog/2011/theotechnos-some-reflections-on-the-intersection-of-social-media-and-theology.

The apostle Paul wrote various situational letters in the New Testament to address specific matters arising in the lives of congregants. The content of his letters is often personalized and detailed, such as in 1 Corinthians 1:10-15 naming specific people in the church like Crispus and Gaius, Galatians 1:6-10 calling out the different gospels being preached, Philippians 4:2 regarding conflict in the church between Euodia and Syntyche, 2 Timothy 1:5 reminding Timothy of his lineage, or Titus 1:5 explaining what he instructed him to do in his absence. Paul does not pen vague letters. Rather, he addresses specific churches, specific individuals, and specific joys and problems because he knew them as a pastor. In the same way, our preaching when coupled with pastoring allows us to be direct in our proclamation. We can be direct because we are in relationship with the people to whom we are preaching. As a seminary professor, I often find it challenging to preach as a pulpit supplier, also known as a *guest preacher*. When I do not have a firm pulse on the congregation, my preaching seems (at least to me) hazy, especially in my use of illustrations and quest for relevant applications. Synthesizing pastoring with preaching provides maximum pulpit effectiveness and straightforwardness.

Pastoral care. We can often learn what not to do by learning from a negative example. In Ezekiel, God chastises the shepherds of Israel for their lack of pastoral care and concern for the sheep. Ezekiel begins his prophesy with these words, "Woe to you shepherds of Israel who only take care of yourselves! Should not shepherds take care of the flock?" (Ezek 34:2). He goes on to explain myriad failures of the shepherds of Israel.

Zack Eswine articulates in *The Imperfect Pastor*, "Pastoral care is mostly presence, being with someone in the midst of what troubles them."[9] If we are not available to people and present with them, we will never know if they are weak, sick, injured, lost, abused, scattered, and vulnerable. In the Gospels, Matthew records Jesus' concern, "When he saw the crowds, he had compassion on them, because they were harassed and helpless, like sheep without a shepherd" (Mt 9:36). Although Jesus is the perfect shepherd and we are not, this verse still reminds us of his attitude toward the sheep that we can imitate. When parishioners feel loved and appreciated, they respond positively in kind. The same principle holds true in preaching. When we genuinely pastor our people, the people respond genuinely to our preaching. Likewise, when we fail to pastor, we fail to receive a hearing.

> When one person is willing to step into vulnerability, it disrupts forever the cycle that traps us.
>
> Mandy Smith, *The Vulnerable Pastor*

Pastoral intimacy. When I served as the senior pastor of a church in Denver, Colorado, we had a number of men who sat idly on the figurative sidelines of the church.[10] Their attendance, when I first started, was sporadic and their engagement with the sermon was minimal. A few of them even designated the Sunday sermon to be their weekly naptime. Others cared more about

---

[9]Zack Eswine, *The Imperfect Pastor: Discovering Joy in Our Limitations Through a Daily Apprenticeship with Jesus* (Wheaton, IL: Crossway, 2015), 191.

[10]See Matthew D. Kim, *7 Lessons for New Pastors: Your First Year in Ministry* (St. Louis: Chalice, 2012), 117-18.

checking the score of the Broncos football game than they did on checking the condition of their souls.

After prayer, I decided to begin a small-group Bible study with this group of church outlanders. This particular group of men shared an affinity for sports and playing basketball, in particular, as do I. We met each week at the parsonage, shared dinner and discussion on a Christian book related to men's issues or a chapter from the Bible, and then headed over to 24 Hour Fitness to play basketball. As we spent time eating meals together in the dining room, opening Scripture in the living room, and guarding each other on the court, I noticed a gradual spiritual uptick in their lives. They came to church more consistently. Their eyeballs were tracking with me in their Bibles during the Sunday sermon. They began to serve the church in various ministries. Some even became leaders in the church over the next few years. This small group became a fraternity of Christian brotherhood. Members of the small group grew very close to each other and even revealed the messiness of their lives. We prayed together. We cried together. We drew closer to the Savior together. In many ways, pastoral intimacy is about discerning which moments to allow others to see the vulnerability and brokenness of our lives. As Mandy Smith says, "To tell his story, God often begins with human limitation—a blank canvas where he can begin creating. . . . When one person is willing to step into vulnerability, it disrupts forever the cycle that traps us, giving us permission to share our fears, creating a space for others to be human and for God to be God."[11]

---

[11]Mandy Smith, *The Vulnerable Pastor: How Human Limitations Empower Our Ministry* (Downers Grove, IL: InterVarsity Press, 2015), 12-13.

The British preacher Ian Pitt-Watson once remarked, "Preaching divorced from pastoral concern is blind. It neither knows what it is talking about nor to whom it is talking."[12] By truly pastoring the members of the congregation, my preaching became clearer and more connected. Pastoral intimacy and preaching interest are symbiotic in nature. Like love and marriage, you cannot have one without the other.

CONCLUSION

Do we love the people to whom we preach, or do we just love preaching? This is a foundational question all pastors and preachers must ask themselves. While it is true that sometimes the sheep bite, we might be unintentionally doing our own share of biting back by preaching devoid of love. Having served as a pastor for nearly a decade, I empathize with your pain. Pastoral ministry is far from easy. I still have scars from the bites. Therefore, I close with Paul's words to the Corinthians, "And now these three remain: faith, hope and love. But the greatest of these is love" (1 Cor 13:13). Pastors and preachers often motivate the congregation toward faith in God and hope in Christ. Nevertheless, as Paul suggests, the greatest motivation for all ministry work is love. Being pastoral and loving are the marks of true pastoring and preaching. Preach as a pastor, and pastor as a preacher.

---

[12]Ian Pitt-Watson, *Preaching: A Kind of Folly* (Louisville: Westminster John Knox, 1978), 58.

8

BEING A PERSON OF
CHARACTER AND
INTEGRITY

■ ■ ■

IT FEELS LIKE EVERY MONTH some well-known pastor falls
into some kind of moral failure. Not only do pastors and preachers
succumb to the more commonplace temptations of greed and sex,
but they also find themselves on other precipices of decay, especially when sinful vices remain unmonitored and unconfessed.
Charles Swindoll writes, "It's not enough to be a good preacher.
Lots of great preachers have failed to make a significant impact
because they lack personal character traits and the necessary leadership skills to develop a respected platform from which to
speak."[1] Preaching ability and charisma are inadequate to sustain
a long-term, fruit-yielding ministry. Being a person of character
and integrity is a constant battle in the pastorate and is something
that warrants preachers' purposeful attention.

The statistics on the lack of pastoral well-being leading to
burnout, depression, departures, dissolving marriages and

---

[1]Charles R. Swindoll, *Saying It Well: Touching Others with Your Words*
(New York: FaithWords, 2012), 46.

families, and moral failure are sobering and even discouraging.[2] One might ask, "Is it really worth it to be a pastor and preacher in our fractured times?"

The Greek philosopher Aristotle once pointed out that communication concerns the triad of three elements: logos, ethos, and pathos. Logos is the content or logic of our message. Ethos relates to our ethics, character, and integrity. Pathos concerns our ability to show compassion for and empathize with our listeners. Each of these modes of persuasion is, of course, important in the task of preaching. However, the goal of this chapter is to cultivate in readers a heightened awareness of the significance of their ethos, character, and integrity as preachers and pastors in a world where well-known and less-known preachers continue to fall into various destructive patterns of sin, which abruptly curtail their ministries and hurt their families and congregations.

PREACHING AND THE CULT OF PERSONALITY

We live in a culture that applauds celebrity and success. Even in Christian culture, we flock to churches and conferences where certain pastors are "known quantities." We may envy pastors of big churches who seemingly have it all: a vibrant, flourishing congregation, a wonderful spouse, adorable kids, a high sense of fashion, conference speaking engagements galore, a steady stream of book contracts, and unending networking influence. The cult of personality drives North American ministry as much as any other industry. We are jealous of the top-dog pastor who

---

[2]For instance, see *The State of Pastors: How Today's Faith Leaders Are Navigating Life and Leadership in an Age of Complexity* (Ventura, CA: Barna Group, 2017).

seemingly answers to no one. Sometimes this type of preacher attracts crowds with heavy doses of humor and light doses of hermeneutics. We picture this influential pastor signing contracts with lucrative advances with noted Christian publishers who are willing to put into print their slightly modified sermon series. While this caricature of a successful North American pastor is just that—a caricature—we still admit that most, if not all, preachers desire sometimes to be a person of recognized kingdom significance.

However, as much as our Christian culture celebrates buildings, budgets, and books, our reward in ministry is not received by establishing an earthly name for ourselves. The work of pastors and preachers is a high and serious calling. The letter of James warns any seeking a pastoral office: "Not many of you should become teachers, my fellow believers, because you know that we who teach will be judged more strictly" (Jas 3:1). We are engaging in valuable work for God's kingdom regardless of who recognizes our names. We should also know that pastors of large and "significant" congregations experience the additional seductions of worldly acclaim. Satan preys, it appears, on megachurch pastors, waiting to devour his next victim. Yet the reality is that every pastor is susceptible to moral collapse. All of us are vulnerable and "prone to wander" from the Lord.[3]

ABOVE ALL ELSE, MAINTAIN YOUR ETHOS

Preachers, strive to maintain your ethos, your credibility, your character. The Bible is replete with verses on the importance of our

---

[3]Robert Robinson, "Come Thou Fount of Every Blessing," 1757.

integrity and character: "Whoever walks in integrity walks securely, but whoever takes crooked paths will be found out" (Prov 10:9). "A good name is more desirable than great riches; to be esteemed is better than silver or gold" (Prov 22:1). Paul instructs Titus: "In everything set them an example by doing what is good. In your teaching show integrity, seriousness and soundness of speech that cannot be condemned, so that those who oppose you may be ashamed because they have nothing bad to say about us" (Titus 2:7-8). Right about now, you may be thinking, *Yes, thank you for sharing these verses, but how can we maintain our ethos in ministry?* One way is to know our finiteness and limitations.

> Not many of you should become teachers, my fellow believers, because you know that we who teach will be judged more strictly.
>
> *James 3:1*

REPEAT AFTER ME: I AM NOT SUPERMAN OR SUPERWOMAN

Two of the greatest challenges in pastoral ministry are the ability to delegate the work of ministry and to maintain self-care. In the church where I served as senior pastor I often felt like "*they* paid *me* to do the work of the *entire* ministry." There are numerous problems with this perspective, but I will comment here on one aspect. It is too easy to fall into the trap of working every single day. The idea of sabbath keeping never quite reaches its actual fulfillment. In *Resilient Ministry*, Bob Burns, Tasha D. Chapman, and Donald C. Guthrie observe,

> Perhaps more difficult than working out scheduling issues for a sabbath is the challenge for pastors to help their congregation understand the need of a day of rest. . . . Because parishioners don't experience this lifestyle, many are simply not aware that pastors don't experience sabbath on Sunday. . . . The result? Many pastors never take a break. This is both disobedient and unwise.[4]

The corollary of routinely missed sabbaths is spiritual, relational, physical, and emotional breakdown. This unhealthy habit of workaholic behavior leads pastors down the path of ministry burnout and moral turpitude. Repeat after me: I am not Superman or Superwoman. To be a person of character and integrity requires self-care. In my years of pastoral experience, I can only count on one hand the number of times parishioners asked me how *I* was doing. Find a pastor's prayer group, seek accountability and prayer partners, join a fitness club and patron it regularly, keep your marriage and family in focus, take your vacation weeks and days off, consume healthy foods, sleep more when your body needs it, find ways to replenish your body and soul. Our sheer fatigue in life and ministry can drag us even unconsciously down the road of moral failure. I have found myself most vulnerable to various sins when I am tired and depleted. Integrity is the concept of being whole. Do not be afraid to say that oddly foreign word, "No!" Since pastoral ministry pulls us in every direction, find your center in Jesus Christ and find ways to bring wholeness to your life.

---

[4]Bob Burns, Tasha D. Chapman, and Donald C. Guthrie, *Resilient Ministry: What Pastors Told Us About Surviving and Thriving* (Downers Grove, IL: InterVarsity Press, 2013), 54.

BE YOURSELF, LIKE YOURSELF

It is a natural human instinct to want what you do not have. Adam and Eve demonstrated this. Instead of being grateful for the 99.99 percent of food and fruit at their disposal, they could not resist the one produce that God forbade them to eat. In the same way, our humanity craves not what God has in his sovereign wisdom chosen for us: perhaps it is our race, ethnicity, skin color, culture, nationality, gender, height, voice, hair color, humor, personality, introversion, extroversion, etc. We often reject God's blessings by focusing on what we want rather than on what we have.

> Many pastors never take a break. This is both disobedient and unwise.
>
> Bob Burns, Tasha D. Chapman, and Donald C. Guthrie, *Resilient Ministry*

In the life of the preacher, similar longings and insecurities come to the surface regularly. We might wish that we could preach like a better-known pastor. We might wish we owned their preaching style, keen exegetical insights, delivery, voice, sense of fashion, likeability, wit, humor, relationality, passion, and other preaching mannerisms. I often tell my students to be themselves in the pulpit. To add to that, like yourself too. Do you like yourself? Warren Wiersbe says, "After all, being myself is the real secret of originality."[5] There will never be another

---

[5]Warren W. Wiersbe, *The Dynamics of Preaching*, 3rd ed. (Grand Rapids: Baker Books, 2001), 143.

Matthew D. Kim. There will never be another you. You are God's workmanship. You are God's chosen preacher. He created you exactly how he wanted you to be with all of your fortes and kinks. Like it. Love it. Live it. Preach out of it.

One of the ways to safeguard your character and integrity is to be who you are and like who you are instead of trying to be someone else or liking who someone else is. Haddon Robinson used to say, "You don't hear a sermon. You hear a person." The entire person of the preacher is the medium God uses to communicate his word. Known ironically to his biographers as a shy, rapidly speaking preacher with stiff technique and poor eye contact, Phillips Brooks, in his Lyman Beecher Lectures in Preaching at Yale, coined the legendary phrase that "preaching is the bringing of truth through personality."[6] One would think that the genesis of such a quote would be the quintessential embodiment of communicative flair!

Nothing changes the fact that we are embodied beings. Our outer shell looks different for each person, and we have unique personalities and idiosyncrasies. Those who can own their sense of identity and being can help others do the same in their own lives. We can learn from other preachers and the skills we admire about them, but the maturing preacher appreciates his or her skills and also recognizes one's weaknesses. We can be free to be ourselves in the pulpit. Preach out of who you are: be yourself and especially like yourself.

I am not a magnificent preacher by any stretch of the imagination. I am not well-known or famous. I know who I am.

---

[6]See Phillips Brooks, *Lectures on Preaching* (New York: E. P. Dutton, 1907), 5.

I accept that. According to one website, statistically 775 people share the name Matthew Kim in the United States alone.[7] I am actually grateful to God for my lack of renown because he knows I probably could not handle fame. Whether people know and say our names or not, a central pillar for faithful and effective preaching entails being a person of character and integrity.

CONCLUSION

While the following words alone are insufficient to keep you in pastoral ministry, I still say, "Hold on." Hold on to God's calling and vision. Hold on to Christ's power and authority. Hold on to the Holy Spirit's reassurance and encouragement. Our treasure is in Christ alone. Paul confesses to the Philippians, "What is more, I consider everything a loss because of the surpassing worth of knowing Christ Jesus my Lord, for whose sake I have lost all things. I consider them garbage, that I may gain Christ" (Phil 3:8). At the end of your ministry, it will all be worth it when you see Jesus Christ face-to-face. If we are blessed to hear these words from God, the Father, "Well done, good and faithful servant" (Mt 25:21), then every earthly sacrifice, every sweat and tear, every disappointment in ministry, every insult and criticism, every word of appreciation never to tickle our ears, every sermon preached, will be worth it. For this to happen one day, continue to cultivate and mature as a person of character and integrity.

---

[7] See "Howmanyofme.com," Auron Technologies LLC, accessed March 22, 2018, www.howmanyofme.com/search/.

BEING PRAYERFUL
AND SPIRIT-LED

■■■

WHEN I WAS A CANDIDATE for my first full-time pastoral position, one of the assistant pastors at the church looked me up and down with his arms folded across his chest. It was an unnerving feeling as we were standing in the church's parking lot. He then pricked my conscience by asking this blunt question, "So Matt, how many hours a day do you pray?" My immediate reaction was one of scoffing on the inside, *Excuse me? The nerve of this guy! Who does he think he is?* However, to tell you the truth, the question stumped me. Good questions can sting the soul. I thought to myself, *Hours? I do not think in terms of hours. I think in terms of minutes.* Instead of answering his question with a quantitative number, I embarrassingly just blurted out something generic, "Of course, I pray regularly." As I continued to search for that first pastorate, however, that question never escaped me, "So Matt, how many hours a day do you pray?"

In asking this very pointed question, God was using this pastor to speak in my life. I was searching for a pastorate in order to shepherd others and to establish a preaching career, but I was not being shepherded by the True Shepherd. I did not have a vibrant prayer life or much of one at all. Three years in seminary and another three years pursuing a PhD left my spiritual life like a well gutted dry. On top of that, as a highly independent person, I often struggle with prayer. That same struggle followed me into my first call to ministry. If I am honest, prayer is still a constant battle.

Most pastors know how to exegete Scripture and how to parse verbs. We know how to find an exegetical idea and a preaching idea for a given passage. We understand how this text relates to biblical theology. We learn about the cultures of the biblical world. We understand for the most part how to relate the text to people's lives. Do we, however, pray for God to transform the lives of our hearers through the power of the Holy Spirit? In short, my answer would be no. I did not *really* pray for myself, for my people, or for my preaching. I was running my life and ministry on autopilot, and maybe you are too!

During my time in that pastorate, Francis Chan published his book *Forgotten God: Reversing Our Tragic Neglect of the Holy Spirit*. Chan's book opened my eyes to massive lacunae in my life, my preaching, and my ministry. He writes, "From my perspective, the Holy Spirit is tragically neglected and, for all practical purposes, forgotten. . . . There is a big gap between what we read in Scripture about the Holy Spirit and how most believers and churches operate today."[1] I believed theoretically in the power of the Holy Spirit. I had read many examples of the Holy Spirit's work in the book of Acts. However, I was not living in the

---

[1]Francis Chan, *Forgotten God: Reversing Our Tragic Neglect of the Holy Spirit* (Colorado Springs, CO: David C. Cook, 2009), 15-16.

power of the Holy Spirit nor was I accessing the Spirit's power in my preaching or ministry service.

Many a preacher today would say, "Of course, prayer is an integral part of my preaching preparation." The question is, What correlation do we see between our prayer life and life transformation in our listeners? I am ashamed to say that it took me well over two years to figure out that prayer is an indispensable part of preaching. E. M. Bounds writes, "The little regard we give prayer is evident from the little time we spend on it."[2] Bounds further encourages us with these words, "Prayer, in the preacher's life, study, and pulpit, must be a conspicuous and all-impregnating force, an all-coloring ingredient. It must play no secondary role, be no mere coating."[3] Yes, I would pray here and there throughout the week for my upcoming sermon. I would pray for my sermon on Sunday morning and as I walked up to the pulpit. Yet did I *really* pray?

> The Holy Spirit is tragically neglected and, for all practical purposes, forgotten.
>
> Francis Chan, *Forgotten God*

In this closing chapter, I would like to share three ways to be prayerful and led by the Spirit in our preaching. Prayer is foundational for the Christian life in general and for pastors and preachers

---

[2]E. M. Bounds, *Power Through Prayer* (New Kensington, PA: Whitaker House, 1982), 47.
[3]Bounds, *Power Through Prayer*, 43.

in particular. I hope that these three ways will remind us to make prayer a more foundational part of our preaching ministry.

PRAY FOR HOLY SPIRIT POWER

We have all experienced the mystery of prayer. It is not an exact science. God can use one-word prayers just as he can three-hour prayers. Preaching in the power of the Holy Spirit recognizes that the Spirit works mysteriously and in ways that we cannot fully comprehend.

In Mark 9, the disciples could not figure out why they could not cast out a demon from a boy possessed at an early age. I can imagine the disciples pointing fingers at each other's inability and impotence. They privately asked Jesus about the reason for their ministry failure. Jesus responds, "This kind can come out only by prayer" (Mk 9:29). In other words, they lacked prayer. Perhaps they were trusting in themselves and resting on their laurels. William Lane writes, "They had to learn that their previous success in expelling demons provided no guarantee of continued power. Rather the power of God must be asked for on each occasion in radical reliance upon his ability alone."[4]

Similarly, I wonder if the same self-reliance occurs among God's preachers once we think we have this preaching thing down. Perhaps we pray a little less fervently today than when we first started. Perhaps we pray a little less urgently after we have found our "preaching voice." Perhaps we pray a little less regularly once we learn the ropes of building a "successful" church.

---

[4]William L. Lane, *The Gospel of Mark*, The New International Commentary on the New Testament (Grand Rapids: Eerdmans, 1974), 335-36.

Unbeknownst to us, our preaching can be like a fully inflated tire that has been slowly leaking its Holy Spirit power.

Pray for the Holy Spirit's presence and power. The same disciples who could not cast out this demon eventually received the power of the Holy Spirit in Acts 2 at Pentecost, and their lives and ministries were transformed forever. Francis Chan writes, "They [the disciples] were no longer timid or confused; they were bold and inspired and began to declare and live the gospel of Jesus through the power of the Holy Spirit."[5] If we are honest with ourselves, maybe we can admit that we have not been living in the power of the Holy Spirit, and as a result our preaching has suffered from spiritual anemia. Pray for the Spirit's power.

PRAY FOR TRANSFORMED LIVES

Second, pray for transformed lives through the working of the Holy Spirit. Ministry ebbs and flows through different seasons. After the initial honeymoon phase, pastors and parishioners commonly experience a lull in vitality. Our congregants' lives are messy. Sins abound. Illnesses spread. Cancer roars. Relationships fracture. Jobs are lost. Death snatches another victim. Depression and pains linger on. We minister in utter brokenness. It is a challenging time to be a pastor, as it always has been.

Yet continue to pray for life transformation in yourselves and in your people. Remember Paul's words to the Christians in Rome: "Do not conform to the pattern of this world, but be transformed by the renewing of your mind" (Rom 12:2). Pray for the Spirit to transform the church rather than clinging to the

---

[5]Chan, *Forgotten God*, 68.

lethal precipice of being corrupted by the world. We often see a lack of transformation in the lives of the people in our congregations, but if we use sober judgment, we might also see this transformational malaise in ourselves.

The Christian life was not meant to be like this! As pastoral leaders and preachers, we can change the world for Christ and his kingdom. We can pray for our congregants to live gospel-centered lives in their homes, workplaces, schools, and communities. We can pray for discipleship, sanctification, and holiness. We can pray for Jesus' love to shine through even the lives of tainted saints. Work your way through the church directory and pray person by person, family by family, child by child. Pray for the Holy Spirit to transform God's people. Pray for transformed lives.

Pray for Congregational Intentionality

Third, pray for congregational intentionality. That is, What is your church's vision? Yes, every church has a vision statement or mission statement. Oftentimes they are very general statements such as Making Disciples or Loving God, Loving People. But are you aware of your church's contribution in reaching the lost in your communities?

What is your congregation intentional about? Being intentional is different than being reactionary. We can minister in reaction to something that happens to us personally or corporately. For example, if a group of homeless people begin to visit your church, you may react to the situation by writing up a church policy on how you will help these visitors. However, being intentional as a congregation means we will prayerfully become proactive participants in God's kingdom. We will intentionally learn about the needs in our community and find ways to meet those needs, whether they are financial, relational, emotional, cultural, or spiritual.

Preaching in the power of the Holy Spirit changes entire congregational visions. Remember the picture of the early church in the book of Acts; they devoted themselves to the apostles' teaching, breaking of bread, prayer, and fellowship (Acts 2:42-47). They gave to all in need. They were observant, intentional, communal, and sacrificial. They put others in front of themselves. They were hospitable, joyful, and praise filled. They were a vibrant expression of the in-breaking of the Holy Spirit's potency in their lives. Congregations today need intentional Spirit-led visions and not just reactionary impulses. Pray that the Holy Spirit will lead your congregation to intentionally live out your unique vision to make a rippling effect on your town, city, state, country, and world.

The Holy Spirit works in mysterious and powerful ways. There is much that we do not and will not understand about the Holy Spirit's person and deity. However, solicit the Holy Spirit's power in your lives and in the lives of your church members. Pray for the Spirit to be present in your preaching and ministry efforts. Pray for the Spirit to transform your heart, which may suffer at times from discouragement and disappointment. Pray for the Spirit to invigorate your preaching with creativity and renewed passion. Pray for the Spirit to melt the hearts of your listeners, who are regularly straddling the world and God's kingdom. Pray for the Spirit to bring back lapsed and wayward souls. Pray for the Spirit to use you and your ministry in ways you never envisioned. Pray, always being reminded by Jesus' words: "If you remain in me and I in you, you will bear much fruit; apart from me you can do nothing" (John 15:5). Preach in the power of the Holy Spirit. Be a preacher who is prayerful and Spirit-led.

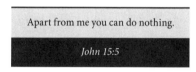

Apart from me you can do nothing.

John 15:5

CONCLUSION

As you pray, trust that God is working through your preaching, teaching, and ministry in ways that you cannot see and do not even expect. I hope that in some small way this book has helped you to reflect more deeply on the importance of preaching and what makes for faithful preaching and faithful preachers. The book is not a textbook nor is it meant to be exhaustive. Perhaps I have not addressed a lingering question for you, or maybe you disagree with some of my homiletical philosophies. However, let me reiterate that we are on the same team. My goal in life is to be a cheerleader for preachers and a champion for preaching.

Even with its skeptics and naysayers, preaching is vital to the life of the church and individual Christians. People's souls and eternities are at stake. Preaching is a privilege. God uses us week after week in the moment of preaching to make disciples who look more like Jesus Christ and to fulfill the Great Commandment and Great Commission in the world. Yes, preaching can be draining and even discouraging at times. Rarely if ever do we immediately see God's transformative work in listeners' lives. We wonder sometimes if they are even listening to us, let alone applying the sermon to their lives.

Yet as you sit down to prepare your next sermon, remember the words of Paul to the Colossians: "He is the one we proclaim, admonishing and teaching everyone with all wisdom, so that we may present everyone fully mature in Christ. *To this end I strenuously contend with all the energy Christ so powerfully works in me*" (Col 1:28-29, emphasis added). You are not alone. Keep honing your craft. Keep preaching.

Haddon Robinson once said, "There are no great preachers, only a great Christ." Therefore, until Jesus returns or calls you home, preach for the love of people and the joy of life transformation, preach with the transformative power of the Holy Spirit, preach for the sake of Christ and the glorious gospel, and preach for the glory of God the Father! Amen.

NAME AND SUBJECT INDEX

SCRIPTURE INDEX

ALSO AVAILABLE:

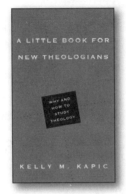

A LITTLE BOOK FOR NEW THEOLOGIANS

Kelly M. Kapic

A LITTLE BOOK FOR NEW SCIENTISTS

Josh A. Reeves & Steve Donaldson

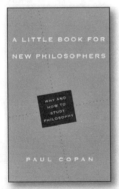

A LITTLE BOOK FOR NEW PHILOSOPHERS

Paul Copan

A LITTLE BOOK FOR NEW BIBLE SCHOLARS

*E. Randolph Richards
& Joseph R. Dodson*